The Story of Parish of Berkswich
(Near Stafford)

WHAT HAPPENED IN THE BISHOP'S MANOR

Part 1
Radford, Weeping Cross, Baswich,
Stockton & Walton

By

Alfred Middlefell

Published by
Berkswich Local History Group

Copyright 1995   Alfred Middlefell

Published by
Berkswich Local History Group

ISBN 0-9527247-0-7

Reprinted 1997

Typeset by: Trent Valley Software
Printed by: Counterprint
              Tipping Street, Stafford

Contents

Foreword by Dudley Fowkes   Page 7
(Staffordshire County Archivist)

Author's Acknowledgments   Page 8

Introduction   Page 9
The Ecclesiastical Parish of Berkswich, being the Manor of the Bishop of Lichfield & Coventry from before 1066 to 1534 when it was returned to the Crown.

Chapter 1: Radford   Page 14
The early history before the river bridge over the Penk, when the Cank Forest, a royal hunting reserve, came down to the banks of the river. The building of the Staffs & Worcs canal in 1744 with the creation of the canal port at Radford. The Hospital of St Lazarus for lepers in the 13th Century.

Chapter 2: Weeping Cross   Page 20
"Weeping Cross Inn" built before 1717, owned by George Badderley, sold in 1813, to be replaced by the "White House". This was demolished in 1850 to build "Baswich House". The history of the Salt family to their departure in 1920. "Weeping Cross House" built in 18th century

Chapter 3: Baswich   Page 26
The early farms. Weeping Cross Farm - early 19th century. The mystery of Baswich Farm.

Chapter 4: Baswich Church   Page 31
The history of the church from the 10th century to 20th century. The Fowler Tomb, The controversy over the Levett and Chetwynd pews. The Lych Gate puzzle. The Trent Valley Railway and the Salt Works.

Chapter 5: St. Thomas' Priory   Page 43
Its development in the 12th century and 'sacking' by the Crown after the Reformation in 1539. Life within the Priory during this period. Use as a centre of the Catholic faith up to 1719.

Chapter 6: Stockton & Walton (1650-1850)   Page 63
The early development of Stockton, the Manor House at Walton. The first Post Office at the 'Springs', St Thomas' Church, - damaged by lightning in 1845. The Salt School

Chapter 7: Stockton & Walton (1851-1921)   Page 80
Walton Garage, Lady Salt and Walton on the Hill, Walton Cricket Club, St Thomas' Church - Building the new spire, The Three Decker, Walton Bury and the National School

List of Photographs, drawings and maps

Plate	Title	Page
Map 1	Radford Stockton & Weeping Cross 1902	13
1	Radford River Bridge built 1825	14
2	Radford Wharf & Trumpet Inn	16
3	The Port in Stafford	16
4	Auction Notice for Railway Property -1814	17
5	Radford Bank 1912	19
6	Baswich House built 1850	22
7	Dining Room in Baswich House School	22
8	War Memorial at Weeping Cross	23
9	Weeping Cross House	24
10	Weeping Cross about 1910 - (Baswich Lane on left))	26
11	Weeping Cross Farm Entrance	27
12	Weeping Cross Farmhouse	27
13	Barn at Weeping Cross Farm	28
14	Baswich "Church" Farm	28
15	Gate between Vicarage & Baswich Church	29
	Isometric Drawing of Baswich Church	30
16	Possible outline of Baswich Church circa 1360	32
17	West Window in Baswich Church	32
18	The Fowler Tomb	33
19	Richard Trubshaw's Sketch for Church (April 1739)	34
20	Plan of Chancel in Baswich Church 1740	35
21	Three Decker Pulpit	36
22	Chetwynd Pew	38
23	Levett Pew	38
24	Reed Organ Baswich Church	40
25	Lych Gate - Baswich Church	41
26	Ladder Bridge at Baswich	42
27	John Teasdale's Impression of St Thomas' Priory	43
Map 2	Layout of St Thomas' Priory	44
28	Seal of St Thomas' Priory	45
29	Slaying of Thomas A'Becket	45
Map 3	Detailing Land given to the Priory upto 1686	46
30	Entrance to Prior's Parlour	49
31	Prior's Parlour	49
32	Medieval Bridge at St Thomas' Priory	50
33	Remains of the North Wall of the Priory Church	51
34	Elevation of North Wall of Transept & Chapel	51
35	North Wall of North Transept & Chapel	52
36	Henry VIII & Seal	55
37	Pillaton Chalice & Plate	58
38	Priory Mill circa 1910	60
39	Stone Coffin & Skeleton	61
40	Baswich Church c 1900	61

Ancient Parish of Berkswich.

Plate	Title	Page
Map 4	Walton 1734 - 1850	62
42	Waterman's Canal Bank Cottage at Stockton	63
43	Stockton Farm	65
44	Manor House (later called Walton on the Hill)	68
45	Thatched Cottages later used as the Post Office	70
46	Wisteria Cottage and 'The Springs'	71
47	Mr & Mrs Woods outside Post Office at The Springs	72
48	Walton Farm	72
49	Three Terraced Farm Labourers Cottages	73
50	Rev HB Scougill 1844-1857	74
51	Walton Church struck by Lightning in 1845	75
52	Salt Dame School for Infants 1840-1894	76
53	Walton Lodge	77
54	Walton National School built 1837	78
55	Mr Thompson's House	78
Map 5	Walton 1850 - 1920	79
56	Cottages on Stockton Lane (looking towards Lichfield Rd)	80
57	Stockton Farm	81
58	Walton Garage circa 1920	82
59	"Walton on the Hill"	83
60	Congreve House (Manor Farm)	84
61	S Wood's painting business at rear of Post Office	85
62	Mrs KH Woods & daughter at Old Post Office	86
63	Thomas Fletcher's Cottage	86
64	Mr Fletcher outside the Smithy	87
65	Miss Tagg's & Mr Bennett's Cottages	87
66	Walton Cricket Club 1886	88
67	Mr Northwood's on Brocton Lane	89
68	Walton Bury	90
69	Hon Mrs E M Allsopp	90
70	Farnworth Brothers' Cottages 1920	91
71	Cottages in Village	92
72	Village Stores	92
73	Village Hall Commitee	93
74	Rev Charles Steward 1857-1865	94
75	Rev Charles Drew 1871-1882	94
76	Replacing the spire on St Thomas' Church in 1903	95
77	St Thomas' Church and Vicarage	96
78	Rev F G & Mrs Inge (1882-1912)	97
79	Mr & Mrs Longson	99

Appendix

1	Assessment of Scrap Value of Baswich Church in 1803	101
2	Inventory of contents of Chapel & Sacristy in 1684-8	102
3	Extract from Constable's Accounts 1701-1736	105
4	Extract from Churchwarden's & Overseer's Account Book	106

Foreword

Local history is a subject of endless fascination. With its associations with medieval monasticism, an early hunting forest and a whole host of local families such as the Pagets, the Ansons, the Salts, the Levetts and the Chetwynds, this statement is as true of the parish of Berkswich as anywhere.

Because of these links with well-documented families and the survival in quantity of official records such as parish records, there is a vast amount of raw material on Berkswich for the historian to draw on and this fact is continually apparent as Mr Middlefell guides us around this first section of the ancient parish.

For a small local history society this publication is a major undertaking and Berkswich Local History Group is to be congratulated for its enterprise.

Dudley Fowkes
Staffordshire County Archivist and
William Salt Librarian.

October 1995.

Author's Note

The writing of this story came about through a set of related circumstances spread over many years. In 1969 I was interested in the remains of the Priory of St. Thomas on the border of the Parish of Berkswich and I was given very willing help by Mrs. Hudson and Mr. & Mrs. Collier whose farms stretched over the area of the Priory remains. Both farmers besides granting me a free hand to roam over their land taking photographs of the remains of the Priory, also told me of items of history which they had collected over the years.

In 1970 I was able to use these and other photographs in the production of "History with Flowers" for the flower festival of the parish churches, then in 1982 I researched 100 years of history through the parish church magazine the "Three Decker" to co-edit the production of the book by that name.

In 1991 James Foley, Youth & Community Worker at Walton High School, got together a small group of the older people of the Parish to enable him to record their memories of earlier years and bring along photographs of by-gone days. He then called a meeting of interested local people and asked if they could, from this small beginning, build up a local History Group.

In 1992 Berkswich Local History Group was formed, and when I commenced a series of talks, Desmond B. Sant, who had in 1949 produced a book called "If Stones Could Speak", passed to me his files of a wide collection of research which had taken him hundreds of hours to collect. It had been his intention to produce another book but he had been forced by personal circumstances to discontinue the work. His outstanding kindness and co-operation in allowing me to use his material has helped to considerably reduce the amount of time I have spent in producing the talks from which this book has been compiled

In the writing of Part One I would like to thank the following :-
Desmond B. Sant for the research material he passed to me which reduced considerably the years of research.
Mr Dudley Fowkes and the County Record Office and Lichfield Diocesan Registry for material given to Mr Sant which has been used in my book.
William Salt Library
David & Nicholas Dodd for their help with my computer.
I would also like to acknowledge the help and advice on many items of local history from the late Mrs. D.R. Haszard.
Thanks to the following for photographs and photographic work:-
Members of Berkswich Local History Group
Mr. & Mrs .Harvey Woods, Mr James Foley, Mr Robin Belcher, Mrs. E. Giles, Mr. D.B. Sant, Mr. J. Pritchard, Mr. M. Woollaston, Mr George Edwards, Mrs Betty Nixon, Mrs Marjorie Knight, Mrs Marjorie Parker,
Mrs Laura Husselbee, Mr Hunt, Mrs J. Lawton, Mrs Joan Pickering, Mrs W Evans, Mr W Weaver.
Mr Robert Morton for very many hours at his computer typesetting and editing the book
Mr Richard Pepper for co-ordination and promotional work
Mr M. Sleightholm and Mr A. Hayward for their work as proof-readers

Mr John Teasdale for artwork
Mr John Smith for artwork
Mr Geoffrey Allen for secretarial work.
My wife Marjorie and many other senior citizens of the parish for much helpful advice
Berkswich Parish Council and Walton Youth & Community Education Centre.

Alfred Middlefell   October 1995.

Introduction

Before the Reformation of 1534, the Church of Rome, through the Bishops, Canons and Priests controlled the lives of the people in the Parishes. The land within the Parish of Berkswich was granted to the Bishop of Lichfield Coventry & Chester before 1066, so in the early days, the Parish was classified as an Ecclesiastical Parish. To explain, let me quote an extract from the parish magazine of August 1957; *"For 1300 years England has been divided into parishes. This parochial system was introduced by the Archbishop of Canterbury, Theodore Tarsus, who was a Greek, to create mutual responsibilities. Every parish priest is given a definite responsibility to his bishop for every soul within the confines of his parish, and everyone in the land is a parishioner of some priest to whom he is entitles to turn for some counsel and help. For 1300 years the parish church and the parish priest have formed a chief rallying point for the people who live around the church."*

From the 16th century until the 19th century, the Parishes were controlled by a partnership of the Church and local Justices. The Church looked after its buildings, spiritual responsibilities, and combined with the Justices in helping the poor through what was known as "The Overseers of the Poor ".

This parish must have been in existence before 1066 and there must have been a church established in it because there is a reference to "the Priest of Bercheswic" in the Domesday Book (1068)

So far we have a priest and a parish so let us consider the name of the parish. Is the parish called Berkswich or Baswich? Baswich is the accepted name of the present day, but in earlier times records show that it has been called Bercheswic, Beswick, and in the old chartularies of the St.Thomas' Priory it was written "Bercleswick". In total there have been eighteen different ways of recording the name since Domesday records. There are of course authorities, who have maintained that the name was derived from a Saxon who owned the parish, but any reference back to Saxon times must certainly focus on St. Bertelin, who was a prince, the son of Queen Ethelfleda, who, you may recall, along with St. Chad, founded the town of Stafford. St. Bertelin, it is said, had a hermitage at Baswich around where the present church now stands.

Let us now look at the extent of the ancient parish. Radford, Baswich, Stockton, Walton and Milford were regarded as one township. (called Baswich). Brocton was regarded as a separate township. Bednall, Acton and Teddesley Hay were part of the parish until 1671 when they formed a separate township. (Some early records show Teddesley Hay as being part of the Cannock Parish, but at some later date was joined to Baswich.) The boundaries were formed by the Rivers Penk and Sow to the west and north, and to the east the boundary runs through Sherbrook valley, then southward across the Chase to an old waymark known as Cank Thorn (near the War Cemetery). It then goes southward, turns just above Huntington, and then swings westward above the boundary of Penkridge, until it again reaches the river Penk at Acton.

In the Middle Ages, the parish was thinly populated, covered in the greater part by forest. The unwooded areas were undrained and the soil was of poor quality. In the Domesday Report it describes the land as lying waste, no doubt due to marauding armies which had trampled the land, possibly driving local dwellers before them.

During the early part of the reign of William the Conqueror there were two occasions when there was local opposition to his rule and an army had to be sent to the area to quash the uprising. The King did have a number of strong supporters in the area who were followers from France, both warriors and noblemen, and as a reward for their loyalty they had been given manors in the area. Well-known names, which appear in local history are Roger of Montgomery, Earl of Shrewsbury, Henry de Ferrers, who became Earl of Derby and owned much land in the area. Perhaps best known was Robert de Stafford, who was the son of King William's standard bearer, a certain Roger de Teoni. Besides holding land in his own right he, and his successors, also held land for the Bishop until the 16th century. The Bishop at the time of the Conquest, had title to all the land in the parish except parts of Cannock Chase, which had been forfeited by an earlier Bishop, but which were restored to the Bishop, in 1290, by Edward I. The Bishop did not build a manor on his land at Haywood, until 1313; before this, his nearest manor was at Eccleshall.

Doubtless the early Bishops were responsible for bringing monks into the parish to save the souls of the poor. The poor who worked the land were called "villeins", who were almost like slaves. They were tied to the lord of the manor for whom they worked and he had to provide them with a cottage and a small amount of land, which they cultivated for themselves in their spare time. Whilst those who had work on the land could be regarded as the less poor, those without work travelled from village to village begging. It was not until the 16th century that a form of Poor Relief was introduced.

The level of crime., in the form of theft and deception, was the area that the Crown thought the Church should tackle by a greater effort to convert the pagans to the Christian faith. The Pope had also shown his concern by sending bands of monks to this country in the 12th century, and the Bishop took six Canons of the Augustinian faith from Darley Abbey to start the Priory at St.Thomas. The extent of their success in converting the local pagans is not known, but the extent of their success in improving the poor quality of the land must have pleased the Bishop as much as it pleased the landowners. Not only did they improve the land of the Priory but they showed their skills in erecting buildings. With the improvement in the land more work was created for farm-workers, but this class of worker seemed to suffer most during the Black Death in 1349, 1362 & 1369. It is recorded that landowners offered better conditions to attract labourers when they had to make up the loss of manpower due to the plagues.

The nature of the parish changed with the disafforestation of the 14th and 15th centuries; and with the increase in agricultural land the population gradually increased. The 16th century. saw a great change take place, which was to affect the lives of people for coming generations. In 1533 Henry VIII married Anne Boleyn, and it was our Bishop, Rowland Lee, who officiated at the ceremony. The Pope declared the marriage illegal, and the reaction was that Henry renounced the supremacy of the Pope. He then introduced an Act of Supremacy to declare himself head of the English Church. The ensuing Reformation resulted in the dissolution of the monasteries, and the closure of the Priory of St.Thomas. It also changed the future of the churches of our parish at Baswich, Bednall and Acton. The effect was also felt by the action of the Bishop in returning to the Crown the land, which for generations, had been held by the church. This, in turn, resulted in the sale of land in the parish to the Pagets, Byrds, Twiggs, and Levetts, followed by the Ansons and the Chetwynds.

A committee, (with the title of "Overseers of the Poor"), which included a member of the aforementioned families, a church warden, a local tradesman and a JP, performed the function in the 17th century which could be likened to our Parish Council of today. (The first meeting of the Parish Council, in its present form, was not until 1894; it was chaired by Capt. W.S.B. Levett.) The main function of the Overseers of the Poor in the 17th and 18th centuries seemed to be to relieve the suffering of the poor, (which involved the building of a workhouse), to maintain the church, to pay for the hiring of pack-horses, and to arrange apprenticeships for orphans.

The problem of crime in these early days was dealt with, one could almost say, by the same committee, who functioned as the Overseers of the Poor, and the accounts of their expenses and of the expenses incurred by the police constables were bound together in the 17th century. In those days the parish would have one, or, at the most, two constables. The job was unpaid, as they were farmers or business men; they were elected on a yearly basis, and were responsible to the Justice of the Peace. They were responsible for reporting any felony, and, in addition, they had to execute warrants and summonses. It was a job very much disliked, and the holder was glad when his year as constable came to an end. An Act of 1842 made it possible to pay the Parish Constable but not all parishes could afford to do so. In the same year the first Chief Constable was appointed.

The parish was not affected greatly by the coming of the Industrial Age. The 18th century saw the improved conditions for travel by road between the towns; not of course the type of roads we know today. Whilst the pack-horse then became a means of communication, it was not until the 18th century that travel through the parish increased with the coming of the stage-coach. A further line of communication through the parish was the canal, brought through to link the rivers Trent and Mersey with the Humber via the Trent.

Even at the start of the 19th century, with more work on the land and more buildings being erected, there were still large numbers of poor people. Church records for that period indicate the extent of the poverty. There were regular gifts of flannel and coal, and records of blanket clubs showed how much the poor had to rely on charity during the winter. Reading the early church magazines one can almost feel how people of the parish lived. The poor were not too proud to seek charity when they were desperate, whilst, at the same time, they made their small contribution for others in need. Some made the supreme sacrifice by giving their lives in the Boer War and the First World War. The sons of the Lords of the Manors also gave their lives as witnessed by the Rolls of Honour in each corner of the parish.

Having given a rough outline of the early parish, I now invite you to come with me on a tour of the parish to learn the more intimate details.

Map 1: Radford, Stockton & Weeping Cross - 1902

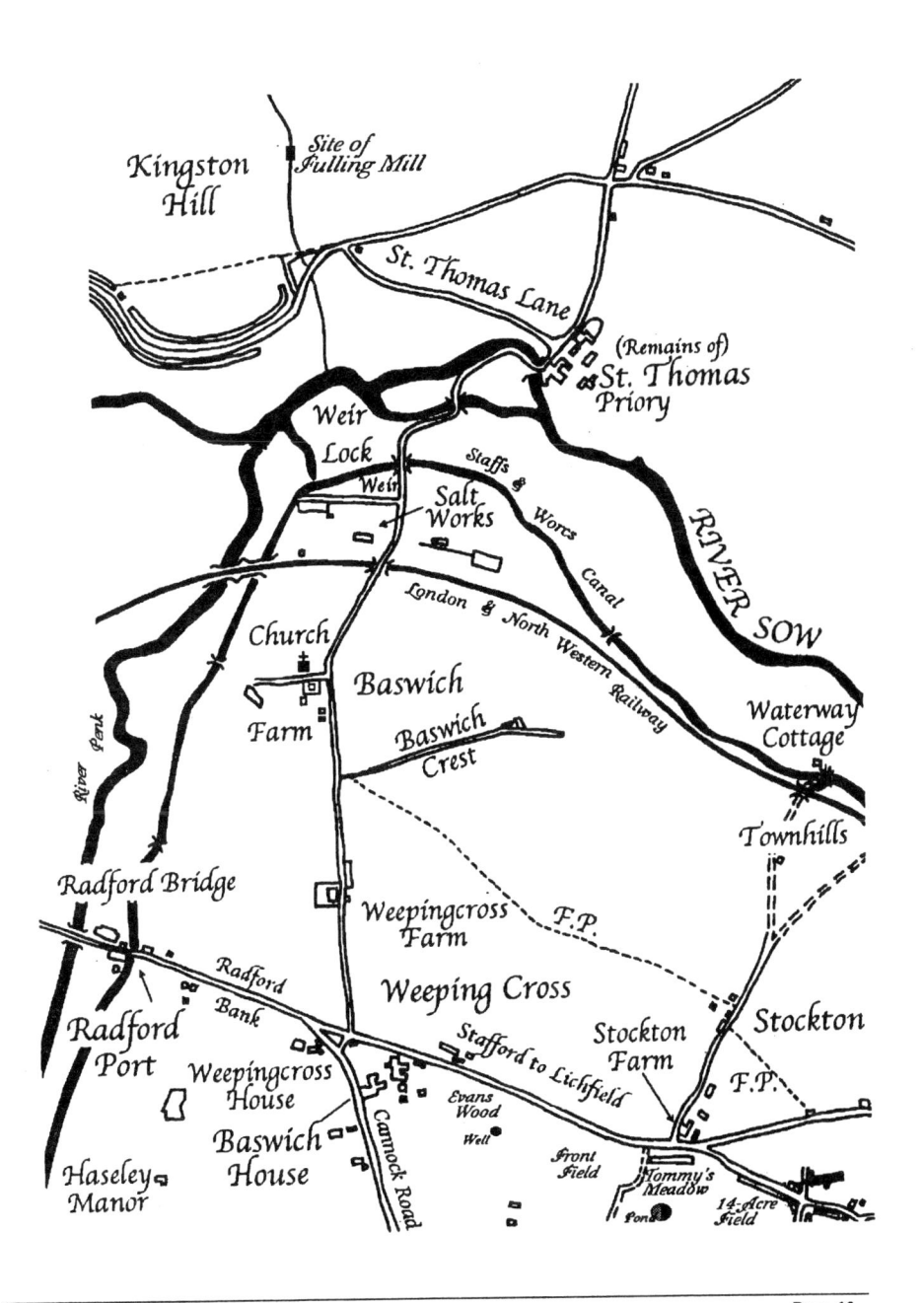

Ancient Parish of Berkswich.

Chapter 1
RADFORD

Let us imagine you are standing on the bank of the river Penk; it is the year 1066 and you are looking towards Stafford. There would not be any buildings to block your view, and, on a clear day, you could possibly see the outline of the town. It is doubtful if you could see much detail, but, when nearer, you would be looking at the Green and at the Greengate entrance to the walled town. It was not until the second half of the 14th century that there is a record of a building appearing between the river and the town of Stafford. This was on the corner we now know as St. Leonard's Avenue, and the building was a hospital known as "The Hospital of St.Leonard". There was a cemetery immediately opposite, now part of the GEC Company. One wonders if this hospital was built to accommodate the poor people who caught the Black Death, which occurred at that time.

However, back to the river, should you want to make your way to Stafford from the bank of the river you would have to cross the ford as there was no sign of a bridge there until 1173. It was built by order of Robert de Stafford, and was, of course, built of wood. It was knocked down and rebuilt again in 1771 and 1799. Accounts for the last rebuilding show the introduction of stonework so one must assume that this was when the first stone bridge was erected. It was again rebuilt in 1825, and the description of that date read "and is of stone ashlar with three rusticated elliptical arches between which are paired Tuscan columns supporting a modillion cornice", which seems very like the bridge of the present day. (See Plate 1 below)

Plate 1 Radford River Bridge built c 1825

It is possible that the rebuilding in 1771 and 1799 became necessary due to this being the era when the stage-coaches started to run, which form of transport continued well into the 19th century. When the railway was brought through the parish on its way to London, it signalled the end of the stage-coaches.

Let us stay with the river, for the church records of the 17th century show that the Overseers of the Poor held their meetings at the "Anchor Inn" at Radford. This was before the canal was brought through, so, by this title, one might wonder if the river in those days was navigable.

Staffordshire & Worcestershire Canal

If we retreated from the banks of the river, before 1766, we could watch that great spectacle of the canal (known as the Staffs and Worcs. Canal) being dug through the boundary of the parish. The project had taken a long time to materialise; for back in 1717 Dr. Thomas Congreve of Wolverhampton had the idea of linking the Mersey and the Trent thus making it possible to transport merchandise across the Midlands by barge. The scheme was taken up by James Brindley from the Potteries, regarded as a pioneering genius of inland waterways. It was not until 1766 that work was started to link the Trent at Haywood with the Severn at Stourport. It was built in a West to East direction, and did not reach Radford until about 1777, and Fradley in 1790. Clay was used to line the canal basin, some coming from Acton, from an area known as Hempits and other supplies from Brocton.

Alongside the canal, which followed the line of the River Penk, was a lime kiln owned by a Charles Dodd, (whose descendants lived in the area until a few years ago), and he provided the lime for the canal engineers. Once the canal was completed, there were only two buildings left between the canal and the river. One was the Anchor Inn and the other was a mill westwards of the bridge. The mill was built around 1173 and was the property of the Stafford family. It appeared in records until 1732. One wonders if the Anchor Inn was pulled down and the first "Trumpet Inn" built on its foundations. The Anchor Inn would have been a suitable name, once the canal had arrived, but it was there in the 1600s before the canal. Then one wonders, why call the pub, which followed, "The Trumpet"? Possibly named during the Boer War (1899 - 1902). This Trumpet Inn was demolished in the 1930s to make way for the building of the present Trumpet Inn, which is further away from the canal.

The Port of Stafford

The first "Trumpet" was only part of the complex which formed what was called "The Port of Stafford".(Plate 2) The buildings and storerooms across the main road opposite were where the barges were loaded and unloaded. There was surprise in those days, when it was found that women worked the coal barges which, on the return journey, took

Plate 2 Radford Wharf and Trumpet Inn

gunpowder charges from an ammunition store, the walls of which were visible behind the rear of the "Shawms" on Radford Rise.

To get merchandise from the port into Stafford, (remembering that in the 18th century the roads were narrow and poor), a railway line was constructed, which followed the road down into Stafford. The terminal was in Bridge Street at the rear of the shops close to the present traffic lights. It was opened on 1st of November 1805. with Mr. John Hughes as manager. In an advertisement in the Staffordshire Advertiser of May 5th 1810 it offered delivery of a whole range of building materials, at reduced prices, to villages within an eight-mile radius. The importance of Radford Port was soon to be diminished when a collection of pit owners saw a better route into Stafford without unloading the barges there. They had a plan to pay for the building of a lock and a weir further up the canal at Baswich, so that the barges could enter the river Sow and sail right up to the Green Bridge. A Port (Plate 3) was built opposite the Brine Baths, this was closed and filled in during 1939.

Plate 3 The Port in Stafford

> **TO BE SOLD BY AUCTION,**
> **By HENSHAW AND SMITH,**
> *At the Star Inn, in Stafford, on Friday the 15th day of July, 1814, at 5 o'clock in the afternoon.*
>
> THE undermentioned Property, viz:—The Railway and Sills between Stafford and Radford, being about a mile and a half in length, laid with Flanch Rails; a capital Weighing Machine, capable of weighing 5 tons, with machine house and blacksmiths shop at the Green, in Stafford; 2 Canal Boats; 2 short River Boats; a quantity of Railway Carriages capable of carrying from 20 to 30 cwt each; a Crane with wheels, &c. and sundry other articles.
>
> For particulars or to view the Railway, &c. apply to Mr. JOHN BARKER, of Radford Wharf, near Stafford.
>
> 17th June, 1814

Plate 4 Auction of Railway Property

Back at Radford, (the railway line having been sold off on 15th July 1814 at the Star Inn, Stafford.), (Plate 4), the Port continued to operate under an agent of the Cannock & District Coal Company for many years. The upper part, at road level, traded as a general stores with living accommodation on the north side. On the opposite side of the road the Trumpet Inn, which sold the beer of a local maltster known as "Salt's Ales", traded under a licensee named Ann Bradbury in 1861. The best known of licensees came in 1904, a Mr. George Leigh. He relied on his sister to run the pub, which had a shop attached on the canal side, whilst he, from a corrugated-iron building on the opposite side, was a cycle-dealer with a repair shop. With the advent of the motor car after the First World War he changed over to repairing motor cars. The present day garage is not far from the spot where George operated. The buildings on the opposite side of the road from the "Trumpet" known as the "The Port of Stafford" were demolished in the 1960s.

Cank Forest

Let us turn our backs on the river and the canal and let our imagination take us back to 1066. All that we would see would be forest, known as "Cank Forest". It was there before 1066, but King William was keen on developing forest lands to raise revenue from their sale, besides providing good hunting for his noblemen. In the forest there were wild boars, falcons, sparrow-hawks and game-birds. There is a lovely description of that age in Sir William Dugdale's book "The Antiquities of Warwickshire". Referring to Cank Forest he writes *"Hugh-de-Loges, (who was one of the King's loyal followers) by the services of conducting the Earl of Chester towards the King's court, through the midst of the Cank Forest, meeting him at Radford, and upon notice of his coming and conducting him through the forest, so if he pleased, he could kill a deer in his coming, and another in his going back, giving him each time a barbed arrow for the hunting."*

"Keeper of the Forest" was an appointment made by the King, and the first, made by William the Conqueror, was Richard Chenvin, the son of a Saxon Lord. Such a prestigious appointment granted to the holder an estate in both Staffordshire (Great Wyrley and Rodbaston) and Warwickshire. The appointment remained with the Chenvin family for many years and then passed to Hugh de Loges, who was deprived of the position in 1246 for poaching venison. Fresh appointments were made every five or six years for various reasons until it was conveyed permanently, with the King's permission, to Philip de Montgomery in 1284. He held it for only 9 years before being gaoled for fraudulence and abuse of his position. It then passed into the Swynnerton family where it remained until 1620. Looking over the whole operation of Keeper of the Forest, there was ample scope for fraud and corruption. Whilst a Crown appointment, the appointee paid the King an annual fee for the job ranging from 10 marks a year, up to 20 marks a year in 1272. This amount they could recoup either from local foresters or from the sale of pannage (pasturage for pigs) and game.

The first mention of a ranger for the forest of Cannock was in 1371. Sometimes they were called bow-bearers, and were appointed by the Crown until the reign of Elizabeth I The last known appointment was in 1560, when Henry, Lord Stafford, was given the appointment for life , "with all the usual profits except for a fee of 6d per day."

There is evidence of royal hunting in the forest in the 11th and 12th centuries. Both William II and Henry I went to hunt there, and it seems that the forest has been a source more of supplies and revenue than of sport. On the other hand the Crown made numerous gifts. The most common were animals for starting other private parks, and wood for building. Wood was sent on one occasion for repairing the walls around Stafford town. In 1244 St. Mary's Church in Stafford received 80 oaks for the repair of the church tower. From land which had been granted to him by the Crown, the Bishop was generally regarded as the most favoured subject, and whilst disputes were common over many years the Crown finally agreed to his claims in 1290. In doing so the area of Cannock Forest having become the land of one person was thenceforth known as a Chase and not a forest. Disafforestation started as early as 1270, and over the years the forests declined in importance; in the 16th century the Bishop returned his holdings to the Crown. By this time a lot of the landscape had been cleared for farming and was purchased by the Pagets, Ansons, Byrds, Levetts, Salts, Twiggs, Hathertons and Chetwynds.

Before we leave Radford, a mention must be made about the Leper Hospital, the exact location of which is not known. The following is an extract from the Victorian History of Stafford :-

THE HOSPITAL OF ST. LAZARUS OF THE HOLY SEPULCHRE RADFORD

By the mid 13th century there was a leper hospital at Radford about one-and-a-quarter miles south east of Stafford. The dedication is variously given to St. Lazarus and the Holy Sepulchre. It was probably founded by a member of the Stafford family for at the end of the century the patronage belonged to Edmund de Stafford.

Little is known of the hospital's endowment or privileges which were evidently meagre. In 1255 Hugh de Doxey granted a moiety of two crofts in Silkmore (in Castle Church) to Walter, Master of the Hospital of St. Lazarus, this land to be held in free alms for ever by Walter and his successors. In 1258 the Master and the brethren, received from the Crown a grant of protection for 5 years.

By the end of the 14th century the hospital's endowments were insufficient for the support of the Warden and the brethren. Edmund de Stafford, patron, attempted to grant the hospital to the Trinitarian Friars of Thelsford (Warws) but his plan seemed to have failed and the hospital probably continued independently for a few years at least. At some time before 1320, William the Prior, exchanged a piece of marsh in Silkmore with Richard, son of John de Wenlock, for a message in Forebridge. This exchange was confirmed in 1320 by Edmund-de-Stafford's widow Margaret and her second husband, and in 1321 by Edmund's son Ralph. Nothing more of the hospital's history is known, and its site has not been identified. There is however, some slight evidence to suggest that it was refounded in the mid 14th century on a new site and with a new dedication.

As we leave Radford and look up Radford Bank, we should consider the gradient of the Bank and wonder how the stage-coaches got up there with a full load. In 1717, which would be about the time that the coaches started to run, the road would be rutted. It was the responsibility of the local people to repair it.

Plate 5 Radford Bank circa 1912

Chapter 2
WEEPING CROSS

Baswich: Weeping Cross Inn
In 1717 there was an inn at Weeping Cross, thought to be on the spot where Baswich House now stands, and it was in fact called "Weeping Cross Inn". It was owned by George Badderley. From the Charity Records he appears to have been a kindly man. He had a brother Richard. From details in these records it would appear that a Mrs. Riley (nee Badderley) owned the inn before George, and she also owned the Mansion House at Weeping Cross. The mystery I have failed to solve is "was Weeping Cross House opposite the site of the inn, built by a member of the Twigg family around 1850, on the old foundations of the Mansion House?" However, back to the Inn, it was apparently a popular meeting place for farmers, and the venue for other meetings, as it was said that 20 or more horses could be seen tethered there on such occasions. It remained until 1813, and from an old manuscript in the William Salt Library we read:-

"To be sold by Auction on the 16th.July 1813 all that large and substantial dwelling house with out-buildings, cowhouses, stables etc., lately occupied as an Inn, and known by the sign "Weeping Cross" may be converted into a desirable residence for a genteel family."

Soon after 1813 the Inn was either rebuilt or converted into a private residence, known as the "White House", by John Stevenson Salt, the first of a great family to reside in the parish. He brought to it not only financial resources for the development of the parish, but also showed himself to be a committed Christian through the work he did for the church at Baswich. He came from the Salt family, who were Lords of the Manor at Standon. He was a mercer in Stafford, but forsook haberdashery to follow banking, in those days a novel occupation, for in those days, 1750, there were only 12 provincial banks in England. He joined the Stevenson Bank in London where he married the daughter of the owner. They moved to Stafford and he joined the Stevenson Bank, which was at the corner of Market Street (now Lloyds Bank). He was appointed High Sheriff of Staffordshire in 1838. His brother William Salt was a noted archaeologist and founded the William Salt Library which was next door to the bank. (now Stafford Railway Building Society). The library later moved to Eastgate Street.

John Salt fathered twelve children, and it was his son Thomas, later created Baronet, who had the White House pulled down, about 1850, and in its place he had built the building we now know as "Baswich House". Sir Thomas added another large room in which to hang 300 beautiful water colours, painted by his mother's brother, J.L. Petit; exquisite pictures in monochromes of grey and browns.

Sir Thomas was a man of the highest principles, and like his father, a great asset both to the Parish and to the town of Stafford. He married Helen Anderton, niece of Cardinal Manning. The first night his new wife arrived at Baswich she was kept awake by a constant stream of people, on foot and in carts, making their way to Stafford. They were all going to see a man hanged.

It was the enthusiasm of Sir Thomas, in co-operation with the Rev. Richard Levett and Lord Lichfield, which brought about the building of Walton School in 1838. Lady Salt was interested in helping the poor and opened the Soup Kitchen in Church Lane. It later became a lodging house for the theatricals who played at the theatre in Tipping Street. It then became an antique shop, before, in due course, reverting to the "Soup Kitchen" Restaurant.

Lady Salt's lasting care for the poor was shown again when, in 1903, an Act of Parliament came into force concerning the certification of nurses and midwives by the County Council. She called a meeting at Weeping Cross House to discuss the advisability of starting a "Nurse for the Parish". She felt that unless people wished to have a nurse and were prepared to pay towards her salary it would be useless to take any further steps in the matter. The proposed scale of fees and annual subscriptions were tabled as follows:-

Class	Annual Subscription	Fees per Week for nurse
1. Cottagers	1/-	2/-
2. Artisans	2/-	3/-
3. Farmers	2/-	3/6
4. Gentry	10/-	10/-

The nurse was engaged at the beginning of 1904 but the above rates had to be slightly modified.

When Sir Thomas died in 1904 the following tribute was paid to him in the parish magazine, "The Three Decker"
" *The parish has lost, by the death of Sir Thomas Salt, Bart. of Weeping Cross, a faithful member of it, a kind friend, and a true neighbour. Brought up from his youth amongst us, he has been to old and young alike a familiar figure -one whose presence we have rejoiced to welcome, whose absence, now that he has been taken from us, we shall greatly feel.* "

On his death Lady Salt left Baswich House and went to live at Walton in the old Manor House which she renamed "Walton-on-the-Hill". She left behind a building described as "An irregularly planned mansion of red brick with oriel windows of wood and many small gables, and is a good building of its period. A single storey picture-gallery and a billiard room had been added by Sir Thomas's son, also named Thomas."

Plate 6 Baswich House

When the Salts left Baswich House it became a preparatory school for boys. (Plates 6 & 7) It closed after the outbreak of the Second World War, and was taken over, for the duration of the war, by Chatham House School, which had been evacuated from Ramsgate. It was also used as an A.R.P. post for the duration. In 1952 it was acquired by Staffordshire County Council for use as a Police Motor Training Centre.

Plate 7 Dining Room at Baswich House School

Let us leave Baswich House by the gateway which was opposite Baswich Lane, (this gateway no longer exists), and look at the triangle of land at the junction of the Cannock Road and the Lichfield Road. before it was greatly altered by road works. It is said that back in the reign of Edward VI a wooden cross stood there where penitents knelt in prayer asking for forgiveness. An old gardener, who worked at Weeping Cross House, used to say that the base from the cross lay in the drive to the house. It still lies roughly in the same spot, and the occupant of the land, where the drive used to run, says *"there is something odd about that stone —it never dries even in the hottest weather "*

On the same triangle of land there used to be a very imposing Cedar of Lebanon tree thought to be many hundreds of years old, and in the 19th century there was a gibbet, a metal cage, said to have been made by the local blacksmith, in which cage the corpses of hanged murderers were placed and left to rot. On the Cannock Road side of the triangle there used to be a black wooden bungalow, which was demolished before the start of the Second World War.

At the very point of the triangle stood a war memorial which was erected on All Saints Day, 1st.November 1920. (Plate 8) It was designed by a Mr. Eden, who was architect for the Wayside Cross Society. In the "Introduction" to this book I mentioned the sacrifices of people, rich and poor alike, who had given their lives in the cause of freedom. I have picked out six names from the name-plates as they or their families appear elsewhere in the book:

Plate 8 War Memorial at Weeping Cross

James L. Cappell. He was the curate at Walton Church until he volunteered for service in 1914. His photograph appears as a member of the "Glee Club". He was popular with the young men of the parish and played for both soccer and cricket teams on the Old Croft at Walton.

Richard Byrd Levett. He was actually the last of the Levetts of Milford, and his sister, Dyonese, married Colonel G.F. Haszard DSO., OBE. A lovely book was published of his letters sent back home during the whole of his war service.

Walter P. Salt. He was a son of the Salts of Baswich House.

Maurice Anderson McFerran. A grandson of Lady Salt.

George Smallwood. The Smallwoods were one of the early families of Brocton (more about them in the next book).

Francis W. Twigg. A son of the Twigg family of Weeping Cross and Walton.

Weeping Cross House

Across the Cannock road from the memorial, one used to be able to see the large stone gateposts, which marked the entrance to the path leading to Weeping Cross House. (Plate 9)

Plate 9 Weeping Cross House

Weeping Cross House was built by the Twigg family. The Twigg family is mentioned in the Domesday Book, but not in the Staffordshire section. They were much in evidence in the reign of Richard II, when the Twiggs from Stockton and Walton were subject to Poll Tax. (This tax was the cause of the Wat Tyler rebellion). Richard, William and Henry also appear in Henry VIII's reign on a Muster Roll. They enjoyed the sport of the Chase and were regarded as excellent shots.

John Twigg, according to the Charity Records, lived at Barnfields in 1745, and Samuel and Roger Twigg, thought to be his sons, lived at Walton at the same time. One must therefore assume that the John and Samuel Twigg, who built Weeping Cross House, were sons of the aforementioned. However the Twiggs, wherever they built, had the reputation of building fine solid country houses. They also built Stockton Farm, Walton Farm, Milford House, (later called Lodge), and Home Farm, Milford. It was no doubt a fine commercial venture when they built the brickworks in Hazelstrine. The house at Weeping Cross had beautiful windows in all rooms with what were described as unsurpassable views. The doors and floors were made of solid oak. Mrs. Twigg was the last of the Twiggs to occupy the house; she left in the early 1900s when Mr. R.P. Ward moved in. The Wards stayed until the 1950s when the house was demolished. John Twigg, who had a share in building the house, died in 1863. Like his neighbours, the Salts, he was mourned and missed by the parish as he had done so much for the local church.

During the lifetime of John Twigg of Barnfields, the church at Baswich went through more than one period of uncertainty. He was involved in the question as to whether the church should be pulled down and moved elsewhere in the parish. During the rebuilding programme of 1739 he used some of the stone to build himself a barn at Barnfields Farm, and added to it some stone from St. Mary's Church to build the entrance to the game-larder, which he put on the north end. His children lived in other parts of the parish, some at the family house, nearby, called "Crossfields". One of his daughters married the curate from the parish church.

Chapter 3

BASWICH.

Let us then leave the home of the Twigg family and make our way across the Cannock Road and the Lichfield Road into Baswich Lane (Plate 10) and, if we look at Map 1 on page 13, it will be seen that on the left hand side there are only two farms and the church and nothing on the right hand side, although three houses were built on the right in the early 1900s. There was a lane leading off to the right which has since been named Baswich Crest. One can now understand why, until the 1950s, it was known as the village without a village.

Plate 10 Weeping Cross c 1910 (Baswich Lane on left)

Weeping Cross Farm
The first farm on the left was called "Weeping Cross Farm". (Plate 11 shows the entrance from Baswich Lane, and Plate 12 pictures the farmhouse itself) It was a large Georgian house and, at that time, it was regarded as a small self-contained village. It was built in the early 19th century, of timber construction with brick infill. The doors, which were of solid oak, had huge keys and bolts. In the front living-area there was a door which, when opened, revealed a bar with a row of china handles to beer pumps, which drew ale up from the cellar. The kitchen had a large coal-burning stove and two hobs, which had to be blackened daily, and on which the kettle was always on the boil ready for a cup of tea. In one attic room there was a big cheese-press and the stout oak beams had hooks in them for hanging hams. There were maid's quarters, cellars, a butler's

pantry, a laundry, blacksmith's shop, a scullery that had huge ovens built in brick in the walls for making bread, and an enormous copper for boiling the clothes.. There was a cheese-room on the ground floor and under the floor was a concealed well. There were three

Plate 11 Weeping Cross Farm Entrance

separate staircases, two of them going up to single rooms. All the rooms had fireplaces, but there the luxury ended. There were no bathrooms or toilets in the house and it was a case of chambers under the beds for use during the night. During the day the toilets were reached by taking a walk round the outside of the house to "three-seater" wooden ones. i.e. three people could sit side by side. They were just holes in the ground with a box frame fitted over them. There were three such buildings located around the outside of the house, and one must assume they were allocated on the "upstairs-downstairs" principle. It was said that it was a bit frightening to go out to them at night as there were no electric lights in those days, and it was not unknown to take someone with you. The only lights were paraffin-lamps, and in the absence of fitted bathrooms, baths were taken in zinc tubs.

Records show that, in 1850, a land owner named William Grindley was in occupation of the farm. Whether he had it built is not known, but, as shown, it was built to provide a standard of living to which no doubt he was accustomed. It was his hope that his son would carry on after him, but when he died in 1884 his son left the farm to take up the manufacture of pottery.

The farm was taken over in 1884 by William Stubbs, who spoiled the appearance of the farmhouse by plastering over the timber structure. He

Plate 12 Weeping Cross Farmhouse

only stayed 10 years, and it was then taken over by an Irish Catholic family named Mullee. They were followed in 1925 by Billy Edwards, who sold it to developers, who planned to build houses. In 1963 the bulldozers moved in.

If we look back at Map 1 it can be seen that there is nothing between Weeping Cross Farm and the next farm (Baswich Farm). What it does not show are the barns and haystacks which stretched almost from one farm to the other. (Plate 13)

Plate 13 Barns at Weeping Cross Farm

Baswich Farm

Here lies a mystery. Old records refer to "The Vicarage" at Baswich, and many have asked over the years where it was. A possible answer was provided by the daughter of the last farmer to farm there. She said that a story had been passed down from previous occupants that, before it was a farm house, it was the vicarage to the church. Some credence can be given to this, for if one looks at the small gate in the wall of the churchyard (Plate 15) it can be seen that this is of a very early age, and is in line with the door of the farmhouse. Could it have been for John Dearle (1741), which could have possibly been about the time of the vicarage being

Plate 14 Baswich Church Farm

Plate 15 Gate between Vicarage & Baswich Church

built? The vicarage moved to Walton in 1841, when it became a farmhouse. Let us therefore think of it as a farm. It was not in the same class of luxury as the farmhouse up the road. It was much smaller but had three storeys and a basement. The only large rooms were the lounge and the kitchen. It had, in the early days, one of the large coal or wood-burning ovens with two large hobs. It was modernised in about 1930, but still had to keep its oil-lamps for lighting until 1945. The lamp, which hung in the lounge, was something special. It was a large brass affair with a glass shade, and its power of illumination so impressed the vicar (Charles Barry), that he asked if he might borrow it for services in the church.

William Foster farmed there in 1851, and it is believed that he was the first farmer after it ceased to be a vicarage. He stayed 10 years, and was followed by Richard Hazeldine. When he left there was high drama whilst Mr. T.S. Hare was the tenant. There was, it seems, an argument between the farmer and an Irish farm-worker, which resulted in the latter being shot. It is said that the stain on the floor, where he fell, stayed there until the house was demolished. After Mr. Hare left in 1892 no tenant stayed more than 12 years. There followed Messrs Gascoyne, Smith, and Yates. During the 1920s the tenant farmer was Mr Joseph Fairbanks.

Mr. Arblaster came in 1932, and, during his time there, the vicar, Charles Barry, used to pop round from the church next door to play the piano and have a "tot". The Vicar was a good pianist, and his wife an excellent cook.

Baswich Farm was reduced almost to a smallholding by 1953, when the landowner started to sell off the land to the developers. So let us go next door to the church.

Isometric Drawing of Baswich Church
Measured & drawn by John Smith

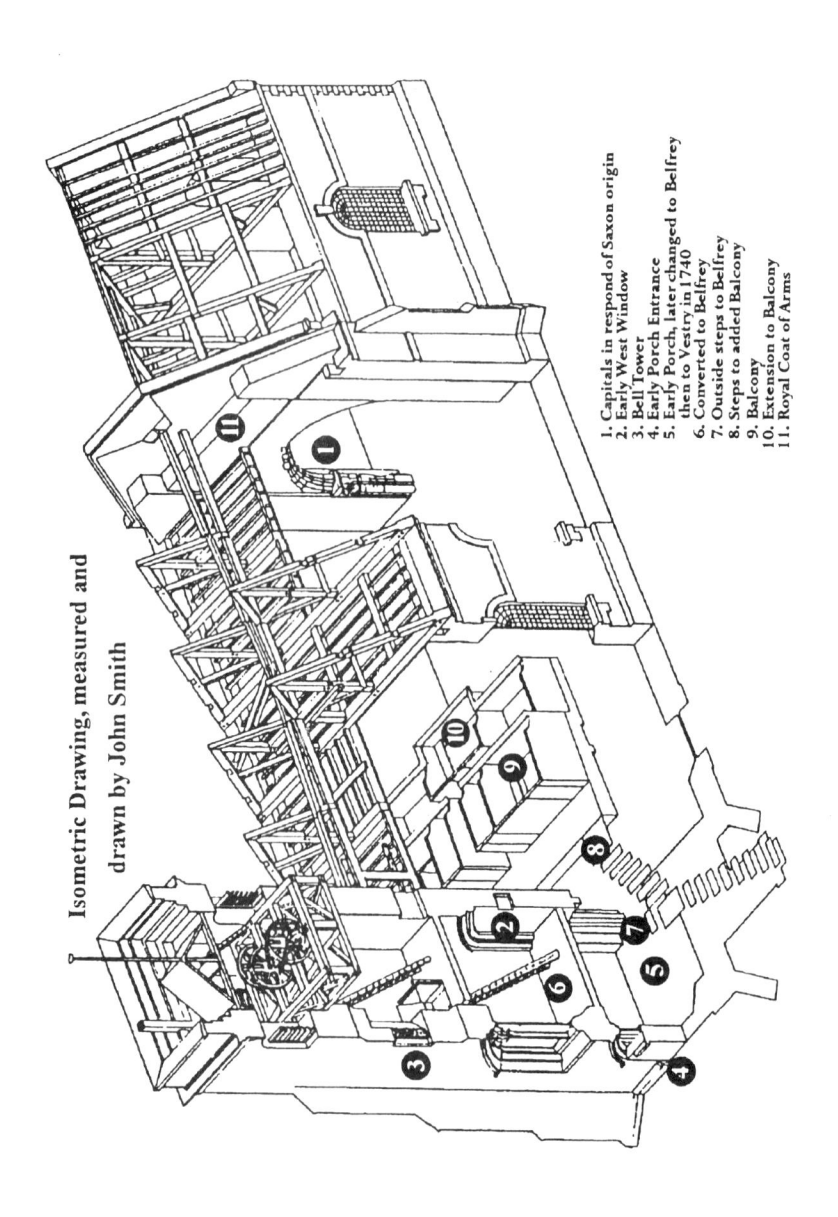

1. Capitals in respond of Saxon origin
2. Early West Window
3. Bell Tower
4. Early Porch Entrance
5. Early Porch, later changed to Belfrey then to Vestry in 1740
6. Converted to Belfrey
7. Outside steps to Belfrey
8. Steps to added Balcony
9. Balcony
10. Extension to Balcony
11. Royal Coat of Arms

Ancient Parish of Berkswich

Chapter 4

BASWICH CHURCH

A question which has been asked many times is *"Why did they build it here ?"* Let us start with a hillside at the edge of the Cank Forest where the land was poor and, as far as we know, unpopulated. The earliest mention of a church appeared in the Domesday Book. According to the legend of the monk Saint Bertelin, he had a hermitage at "Berkelswic", and, if he *was* in the vicinity at the time of his mother Queen Ethelfleda, when she led the Mercian forces to defeat the Danes at the battle of Tettenhall in 910AD, we must assume that the date he was here was in the early 10th century. That seems in line with the Saxon stonework in one of the responds (half-pillars) to the chancel arch. It is however more than likely that the first "church" started with just a wooden cross in the ground, and an early church, built of wood by the monks, followed. This was later converted into a stone building. A similar early church, also credited to St. Bertelin, was built at the west end of the present St. Mary's church and it is thought that this also started with just a wooden preaching cross. It is well to remember, when assessing the life of church buildings, that there is always a clue from a custom, which has always been adopted, that some part of the old church is somewhere incorporated in the new one.

Assuming that the first church was built in the Saxon period, it would then seem that the church was rebuilt between 1086 and 1135, which would account for the Norman stonework in the chancel pilaster. (No 1 on the Skeleton opposite)

From records, it would appear that the church was rebuilt again around 1360 (the Perpendicular period see Plate 16). It would differ from the present outline in that it did not have a bell-tower. Archaeologists Reports also are of the opinion that the chancel-arch at this period was possibly the third, the arch in the Norman period being a smaller arch. The west wall of the church had a large beautiful window, (No 2 on skeleton) below which was the porch forming the church entrance. The small Norman window at the west end of the present church could have been the porch doorway, (No 4 on skeleton and plate 17) for it has been found that the floor of the church in this period was two feet below the present level. In this age it was said that the poor, who sat in the nave, sat on the floor, except for the weak and suffering, who were on a shelf-type seat in the wall. (Perhaps from this arose the saying "the weak go to the wall").

If one stops for a minute to think of the church at this time (1404), it can be seen that in 3 years they had three priests, William Dyngell, Hugh de Hopwass (Presb) and John del Croftes, the last leaving in 1407. It has to be remembered that a short distance away was the Priory of St.Thomas, which had its own church. As one might say, they were not good bed-fellows at this time, as there was disagreement over the apportionment of the

Plate 16 Possible outline of Baswich Church c 1360

tithes received between the monasteries and the English Church. There was no population around the church, as there was at Walton and Brocton where the scant scattering of people lived. (By the year 1563 they numbered only 46).

After John del Croftes left, Bishop John de Burghill, the Bishop of Lichfield, appropriated the church to the Priory of St.Thomas in 1407 and allowed them to serve it either by a suitable secular chaplain or by one of their own number. There are no records to show what happened to the church during the next 196 years, but when it was handed to the Protestant Church in 1603 (post the Reformation) it could be seen that they had done a lot of rebuilding, starting as early as 1407, when the church was taken over.

One must assume that it was the monks from the Priory who did the rebuilding, and time alone showed that they did not have the best building skills. A bell-tower had been built in front of the west window (No 3) and the window (No 4) had been filled in. (The outline of this can still be seen today from the ringing chamber). The foundations of the tower it would seem, were inadequate for the weight of the tower. One wonders if in fact the foundations were the old foundations of the porch, which made it necessary for the tower to be rebuilt at a later date.

During this period when the church had been handed over to the Priory, the patronage had been handed to Roger Fowler of Broom Hill in Norfolk. The three bells found in the bell tower, showed by the markings thereon, that their origin was in Norfolk. It therefore seems that the Fowlers brought the bells with them. It appears that there were initially two bells, with the third arriving in 1591. Records show that a third bell had to be repaired, and was a gift from Walter Fowler, shared with Walter Povie and Matthew Mynors.

Plate 17 Early Porch Entrance

It was also during this same period that the Fowlers built their tomb under the floor of the chancel, and indications are that it was commissioned by Walter Fowler.(Plate 18) Not only the remains of the Fowler family lie below the chancel, names other than Fowler indicate that daughters of Fowlers, who married local people, were interred there. Although the Fowlers, who were recusants, made the Priory the centre of the Catholic faith for several generations, they claimed the right to burial in the parish church.

Plate 18 The Fowler Tomb

We can now look at the condition of the church fabric before the important rebuilding programme of 1740. But before doing so let us go back into the church, before it falls down, and look at the chancel arch. About 1600 there was a wall-painting, above the arch, of a Royal Coat of Arms (Number 11 on the "skeleton"). The painting was carried out in gold, and detailed in red, on a white background with a lion and unicorn supporting a crown and shield. On each side of the crest were the initials C.R ("Carolus Rex"). This was thought to have been either Charles I or Charles II. There would, originally, also have been a garter bearing the legend "*Honi soit qui mal y pense*" plus a motto "*Dieu et mon Droit*". It is thought that the lower part of the painting was destroyed during the rebuilding in 1740, when the roof above the nave and the rest of the church was rebuilt. Today none of the painting is visible.

In 1733 the church was in a dangerous state of decay. The bell-tower was too heavy for its foundations, which were only 7 inches thick. The clamps, which were holding the tower together, were loose, and could be plucked out with one's fingers. The walls of the body of the church were bulging at the foundations, and the timber of the roof was so rotten that it was in danger of falling down. On the 25th April 1739 Richard Trubshaw, Master Builder of Great Haywood, submitted a drawing (Plate 19) with an estimate of the cost of rebuilding. It will be noted that there was a Priest Door in the chancel.

Plate 19 Richard Trubshaw's Sketch for the New Church in April 1739

It was considered that the inhabitants of the parish could no longer afford to raise the sum of £1695 12s 1d.for rebuilding. John Dearle, the vicar, together with John Hodgetts, Walter Chetwynd, Edward Byrd, John Smith, Michael Harding, Richard Styrch and Samuel Twigg (you will remember mention was made earlier in the book of the service some of the above gave to the church) instructed Robert Hodson and Christopher Ward (solicitors, no doubt) to apply to Staffordshire Quarter Sessions for help. After hearing the evidence, the magistrates appealed to the Lord High Chancellor that the parish be authorised to make a national appeal for funds to rebuild the church. A certificate was granted, and Mr. Robert Hodson was appointed collector. The appeal was laid before every parish in the country and, whilst there is no record of the amount raised, the churchwardens at a meeting of May 9th 1739, unanimously agreed that any shortfall would be met by a pound levied upon all the lands in the parish.

Eventually the rebuilding started to a Georgian design, retaining the base of the 15th century tower, extending it upwards from the top of the angle buttresses and surmounting the top with four ornamental weather-vanes shaped like Grecian urns, which had to be removed some years later when they became unsafe. The walls of the nave and the chancel were built in red brick, and the stonework from the demolished church, which became surplus, was bought by the Twigg family, who used it to build a large barn at Barnfields on the Cannock Road. As to the interior, the floor of the nave was raised about 6 inches to be level with the floor of the chancel. The belfry at the foot of the tower, which had previously been the porch (See 'Isometric Drawing at page 30 - No. 5 on the drawing), was converted into a vestry and the ringing chamber moved one floor up (No. 6 on the drawing). This entailed the construction of stone steps to the outside south base of the tower, to reach the belfry or ringing-chamber (No. 7). During this rebuilding a balcony was added at the west end. This was not part of Richard Trubshaw's contract, but was paid for by a John Hodgetts who wanted more space for his family and servants (No. 9). It became necessary to build stone steps to the wall of the tower, with a door in the west wall, to gain entrance to the balcony (No. 8).

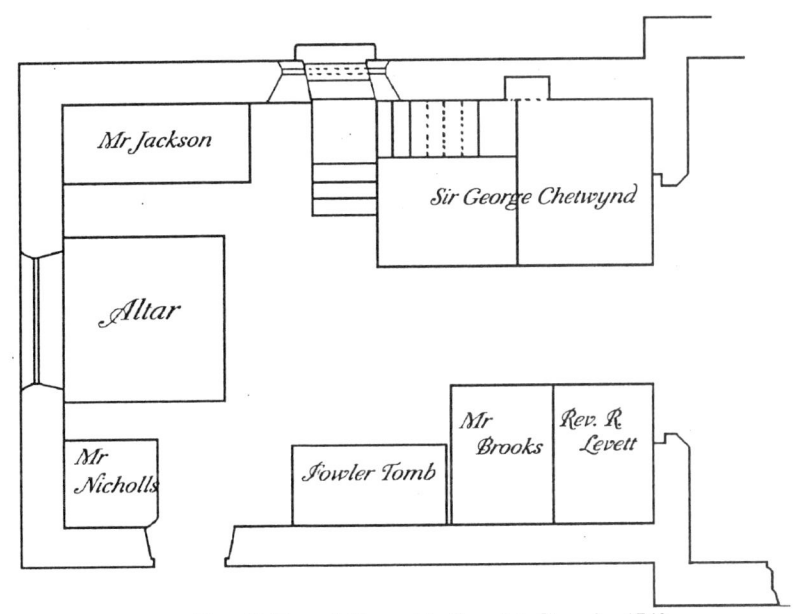

Plate 20 Plan of Chancel in Baswich Church - 1740.

In the body of the church, high wooden pews were installed, with locks on the doors, and from the plan of the lay-out of the chancel (Plate 20)., it will be seen that there was one of these pews at each side of the altar. The two pews opposite each other at the start of the chancel were rented by the two Lords of their respective manors, the Levetts and the Chetwynds. (These two pews formed the basis for a future controversy.) The pew-holders paid a rent for them. The pew rolls for the period contained the names of those previously mentioned plus the names of Morgan and Inge. No doubt the vicar wanted to see what was going on in the tall pews, which resulted in the three-decker pulpit being built. In the specifications for the pulpit it stated that there was to be a sound-board above the pulpit, which was common in those days.

For those who have not seen a three-decker pulpit, perhaps the photograph left, (Plate 21) will illustrate the concept. The Vicar climbs up the steps to the top, from where he speaks, and below, on the second deck, sits the Parish Clerk. There was a wonderful description by an eighteenth-century writer which could fit our Parish church. He wrote :- *"The Squire will allow no-one to sleep during the sermon but himself"*. The Parish Clerk at his official desk, was as prominent a figure as the Vicar above him. On Sunday the Parish Clerk marked the lessons, psalms and collect for the vicar, helped him with his robes in the vestry, and then rang the final tinkling of the church bell, at the sound of which, the men, most of whom had remained talking in the churchyard, trooped in, and the service began. Not a voice was raised in confession, psalms or responses except those of the Vicar and the Clerk. The contrast between the cultured voices of the former and the bucolic tones of the latter fell strangely on the ear. On Sundays when the Athanasian Creed was read, the Clerk made sad havoc of the unusual words. On one such day, the Vicar, to relieve his feelings, said to the Parish Clerk after the service, *"you did not study the Athanasian Creed"*. *"No sir, I didn't"* was the reply. *"But it is a beautiful creed"*. At the close of the prayers and litany, for the latter was never omitted, and after the Ante-Communion service, the Clerk migrated to the singing pew, and the Vicar went to the vestry to change his surplice for the black gown. The Parish Clerk, and never the Vicar, gave out the rare notices, and on one occasion, on being instructed to announce that there would be no service next Sunday as the Vicar would be officiating in the next parish, he stated "there will be no service next Sunday as the Vicar is going on a fishing trip in the next parish". Arriving at the singing pew, the

Plate 21 Three Decker Pulpit

Parish Clerk gave out the psalm with the words, *"Let us sing to the praise and glory of God the hundredth psalm"*, the one very often chosen, and then :-

> *"All people that on earth do dwell,*
> *Sing to the Lord with cheerful voice"*

A note or two was sounded on the pitch pipe, and then the singers, small in number, without any boys or girls among them, began the tune. The congregation rose, and you could see by their moving lips how, inwardly, they were joining in the music, but not a word escaped from their mouths. When the psalms ended, the sermon began, and was listened to with great attention for about three quarters of an hour. There was no collection at the close of the service as the small expenses were met by the church. On Sacrament Sunday, which was confined to the main festivals of the year, a number of old people remained, as the solemn service was held for those who were approaching the grave. The offerings from this service were for the poor of the parish. Such was the village life in the nineteenth century. Times have changed and we have changed with them. A demand sprang up for brighter services and more music, so hymn books were introduced and surpliced choirs, evening services and lighted churches. In the midst of all the changes, the Parish Clerk lost first one, and then another of his rights, until today, where the office of Parish Clerk still exists, he is no more than a shadow of the former importance of his office.

As regards our own "three-decker", it is reported that on one occasion the floor of the top deck gave way, and the preacher disappeared. I wonder what the sermon was about?

The rebuilding of 1740 could not be claimed as a success for, 68 years on, it started all over again. In 1808 the Vicar, the Rev. William Inge, together with the churchwardens and parish elders suggested that the church should be pulled down and built elsewhere. Sir George Chetwynd, in a letter to the Parochial Church Council (PCC), pointed out that the church in its present position meant that many poor people from Walton and Brocton could not travel to Baswich, and a more central position should be sought. An assessment was made by a Mr. Varley (Reproduced at Appendix 1) of the value of the scrap material if the church were pulled down. It amounted to £277.6.4d, which it was said would help to meet the cost involved in building a church elsewhere. Also they could sell a sufficient part of Deepmore Common. In addition Sir George, if the plan were adopted, would donate the sum of, not less than, one hundred guineas, in addition to giving his share of Deepmore. Nothing from this plan seemed to materialise, but it could have sown the germ of an idea that a Chapel-of-Ease could be built at Walton. Sir George Chetwynd, ever mindful of the plight of the Brocton people in getting to church, offered them the use of one of the rooms at Brocton Hall for services, until he could get for them a Mission Room in the locality. Some of the Brocton people were ferried to the church at Baswich by horse and dray belonging to a local farmer named Smallwood.

Nothing happened for the next four years, and then, in 1812, Sir George Chetwynd applied to the Dean of the Cathedral Church of Lichfield for a faculty to erect a gallery over their present pew in the chancel, to be paid for at his own expense. He pointed out that there was insufficient room for his family and servants, and that his standing in society would be sufficient to obtain approval for the project. At the same time, occupying the pew opposite in the chancel, the Rev. Richard Levett made a similar application, but, in this case, it meant cutting away part of the Fowler tomb. Both faculties were granted.(Plates 22 & 23) In the case of the Chetwynd gallery pew, there was real luxury, a fireplace, carpet and an upholstered leather armchair.

Plate 22 Chetwynd Pew

This idea of adding further pews to make more room for families of the gentry seemed to have spread, for, in 1822, a small body of local gentry, no doubt aware of what Mr. Hodgetts had done earlier for his family, decided that they would like to have further pews built on to the front of the existing gallery. A faculty was applied for, and granted, in the names of John Stevenson Salt (Baswich House), John Twigg (Weeping Cross House), Henry Webb, Robert Hanbury, and the Vicar, Joseph Ellerton.(No 10 on Skeleton Drawing)

When they were completed and the gentry took their places for Sunday Morning Service, the extension was seen to have only three pews. John Stevenson Salt sat on the south side, Harry Webb on the north side, and John Twigg in the centre. One wonders how Viscount Anson and

Plate 23 Levett Pew

his family felt when they lost their ringside view of the proceedings by having Harry Webb and his family placed in front of them.

It was not long before the Vicar began to receive protests, but not from the Ansons. It will be recalled that, in the earlier chapter on Weeping Cross, it was mentioned that John Salt raised a large family, and could easily fill his new pew, and it is recorded that when Samuel Salt wanted to share the pew, John was not in agreement. Their dispute, so it was said, remained a problem for the Vicar until his death, after which the Vicar's wife, Mrs. Ellerton, gave up their family pew, which was in the original part of the balcony, and it was granted to Samuel Salt.

All these creature comforts were a bit too much for the poor of the parish who sat in the nave and shivered. Almost from the first these pews on stilts in the chancel were hated by the whole parish and whilst, after some years, the Levetts offered to have theirs removed, there was no similar matching offer from the Chetwynds. The pew of the latter stood unused from 1920 when the family moved away; the Levett pew remained until the rebuilding in 1967 when it was moved into the new extension of the north transept.

The problem of meeting the spiritual needs of the growing population, mainly in Walton, Milford and Brocton, was constantly under review. In 1842 the church at Walton did materialise, thanks to the Earl of Lichfield, who gave the ground, and the Rev. Richard Levett and Mr. Salt, who both subscribed to the cost of materials.

But let us return to Baswich. Although Walton people now had their own church, it was common in those days for some people to go to church three times on a Sunday. The Lords of local manors took up their seats at Baswich regardless, so once again the question of improving and renovating the church was considered in 1846. Whilst a little cosmetic work was done there were again suggestions that the church should be demolished, except for the east wall, and a small chapel built adjoining the tower, which would be used for funerals.

No further work was done until 1899 when the church was altered to almost as you see it today. Out went the tall pews at the side of the altar, and, whilst a further attempt was made to get the gallery pews in the chancel taken down, the Chetwynds would not give way. Work was done on the floor and the chancel arch, but the great thing for the comfort of the people, was that, (excepting the fireplace in the Chetwynd pew), heating was installed for the first time. This meant building a boiler-house on the north-west corner of the church, and, at the same time, the wooden porch at the other end of the north wall was dismantled and replaced with a brick structure.

The next most important thing in the life of the church, was the work done on the east

Ancient Parish of Berkswich.

end, when north and south transepts were added in 1968. This, being modern, is outside the scope of this book., but during the alterations the builders discovered below the floor 12 medieval tiles. They are of 15th century origin, no doubt from the early church.

Plate 24 shows the reed organ from the 1950s, which had to be hand-pumped until it was later fitted with an electric blower. It was destroyed by a fire started by vandals during the 1968 alterations, as was the Chetwynd pew. (They got rid of it at last!)

As we move outside, a look at some of the gravestones reminds us of the stalwarts of the church in years past; men like Thomas Salt, John Twigg, Henry Twigg, John Box. There is a certain amount of pathos and tragedy on some stones. Richard Burton, a shepherd from Acton Hill, and his wife Mary, lost seven sons and one daughter, aged between 2 and 22, in the space of five

Plate 24 The Reed Organ Baswich Church -

years. Five of the children died within the space of 11 days. The epitaph reads "*The angel of death was rampant*". Small wonder the occupants of the farmhouse claimed strange experiences -footsteps without any feet, and the crying of a baby without any baby there. There is also a stone belonging to Thomas Vaul, who died in 1840, which reads

> "*Like me my friends, you too must die,*
> *This life is short and vain,*
> *Oh may we meet in bliss on high,*
> *No more to part again*".

There was another, which has since disappeared, but the story of it lingers on. It read :-

> "*This world is like a city full of crowded streets,*
> *Death is the market place where we must all meet,*
> *If life were merchandise that men could buy,*
> *The rich alone would live and the poor would die*"

When we arrived at the church in our story, in the 10th century, there was no Lych Gate. That was erected in 1894 by Mrs Spooner in memory of her husband Judge Spooner, (of Walton Lodge), who is buried in the churchyard. (Plate 25) As you leave the churchyard the inscription says "*Through the grave and the gate of death.*", and on the other side, when you enter, it reads "*The house of God, the gate of heaven.*" Is it the wrong way round?

Plate 25 Lych Gate Baswich Church

If we turn left as we come to the road we will make our way to St.Thomas' Priory. If we stop to think, when the monks had the church they would be able to see the Priory from here, since the railway and the canal were not there in those days.

LONDON AND NORTH WESTERN RAILWAY (Trent Valley Line)

As mentioned earlier, the canal came through the parish about 1777; the railway through the parish was completed by 1847. Notice was given in the press that as from 1st December 1847 there would now be through trains on the London & North Western Railway to London, instead of the longer route via Birmingham. The new line was called the Trent Valley Line, and it would shorten the journey to Rugby by 11 miles. It was found to be difficult to lay a track over the boggy ground to the north-east of the parish -- it was called a bottomless pit-- so they ran the track over a wooden viaduct. There is a story which tells of a train approaching the wooden viaduct, when the driver saw it was on fire. The driver decided to make a dash to cross before the bridge collapsed. After that they christened him "Hell Fire Jack". The bridge was later replaced with an iron structure, which also spans the canal.

The account of the official opening of the line in the "Staffordshire Advertiser", dated 26th June 1847, reads:- "*The bells of St. Mary's were ringing, flags and banners flying over the station, important guests were assembled and the train was scheduled to leave at 12 noon. It was 20 minutes late in leaving and when it turned from the Grand Junction Line into the Trent Valley line, it was greeted with acclamation. It continued a*

steady and rapid course through the beautiful valley towards Shugborough. Guests were picked up all along the route at Colwich, Rugeley, Lichfield and Tamworth, where it collected more guests from the London train. We are told that the guests totalled 600, the chief guest being Sir Robert Peel. Among other notable guests were Viscount Sandon, the Hon. Colonel Anson MP and Viscount Ingestre. Tables were supplied with every suitable luxury and wines included champagne, claret, moselle, port and sherry."
(In 1923, after the amalgamations, the name of the railway became The London, Midland and Scottish Railway.)

Salt Manufacturing at Baswich.

We continue our journey beyond the railway bridge. To the left hand (north) side of the road between the railway and the canal stood the open-pan salt works built at the end of the nineteenth century by the Stafford Salt and Alkali Company. The S.S. & A. Co. already had an open pan works at Stafford Common from where brine was pumped through a 6 inch main to the Royal Brine Baths, thence alongside the River Sow, crossing the river by Ladder Bridge (Plate 26), to the reservoir at the Baswich Lane site.

By the 1950's the open pan plant had been replaced by a new vacuum plant, built on the opposite side of the lane on what is now 'The Saltings'. This new plant was closed in the mid-1960's following a ban on brine pumping, which was held to be the cause of subsidence to property in the North End of Stafford.

Plate 26 Ladder Bridge in 1931

Chapter 5
ST. THOMAS' PRIORY

As we follow the winding lane from the church the remains of the Priory come into view. Mostly what one sees are the buildings, which have been built upon the stone walls, which were all that remained of the Priory after it was "sacked" by the Crown commissioners in 1539, following the Reformation. We can look at all the details of this later in chronological order. But first let us look at the reason for its being here.

Plate 27 Artist's impression of St Thomas' Priory

Since the days when the Angles and Saxons invaded this country, around 450AD, and drove the early Christians into the hills of Scotland and Wales, it had been the constant endeavour of the Church of Rome to rebuild the belief in Christianity in this country. When William I conquered these islands in 1066, he asked the Church to tackle the problem of lawlessness and theft, which were rife amongst the pagan population.

Pope Alexander came here from Rome in 597 AD for the same reason and, after his visit, there followed various orders of monks, which settled in different parts of the country.

Map 2 - Layout of St Thomas' Priory

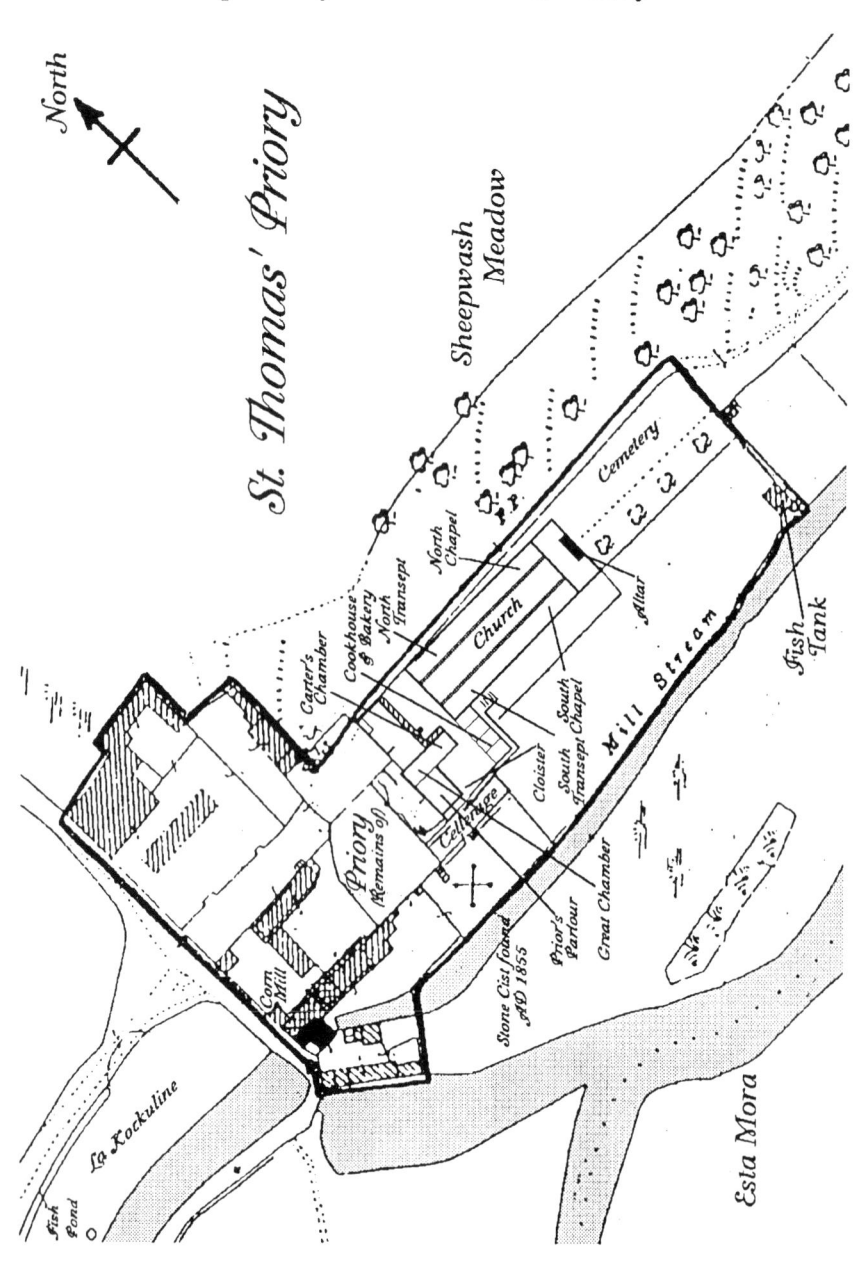

Northumbria was a centre from which monks spread to parts of the Midlands. St. Chad came from there to establish a centre at Lichfield and was appointed Bishop in 669 AD. Monasteries were set up at Burton, Tamworth, Coventry, and in the 10th century, it is said that St. Bertelin set up a hermitage at Baswich.

In the 12th century the Bishop of Lichfield and Coventry, Richard Peche, who owned the land at Baswich, in association with a local burgess named Brian de Stafford, brought six Black Canons of the Augustinian Order from Darley Dale to start the building of the Priory. These black Canons were both "monks" and "regulars", and there were also different orders of monks (seculars) in Stafford. They were the "Grey Friars" at the north of the Town, and the Augustinian monks in the vicinity, which we now know as Friars Road.

Plate 28 Seal of the Priory

Gerardus de Stafford, son of Brian it would seem, had a right to the land from the Bishop, and it was he who started the building in 1174. Plate 28 shows the Seal of the Priory, which reads *"Sigill Coe Prioratus Sci Thome Martiris Juxta Stafford"*.

It would seem that the Bishop at this time, had his attention focused elsewhere, for he, as Chaplain to King Henry II, had become entangled in the quarrels between the King and the Archbishop of Canterbury, Thomas A'Becket. During a period of estrangement between the two, Richard Peche had to stand in for the Archbishop and conduct the marriage of the King's second son. It was said that this contributed to the death of Becket, for which Richard felt some guilt. It was whilst Henry was in France with some of his barons that news came to him of further insults from Becket. This, it seems, was the "last straw" as they say, and, unbeknown to the King, certain of his barons crossed the Channel and slew Becket in Canterbury Cathedral .(Plate 29) In remorse, King Henry sought to have Becket canonised in 1173.

Plate 29 Slaying of Thomas A'Becket

Ancient Parish of Berkswich.

Map 3 - Detailing Land given to the Priory upto 1686

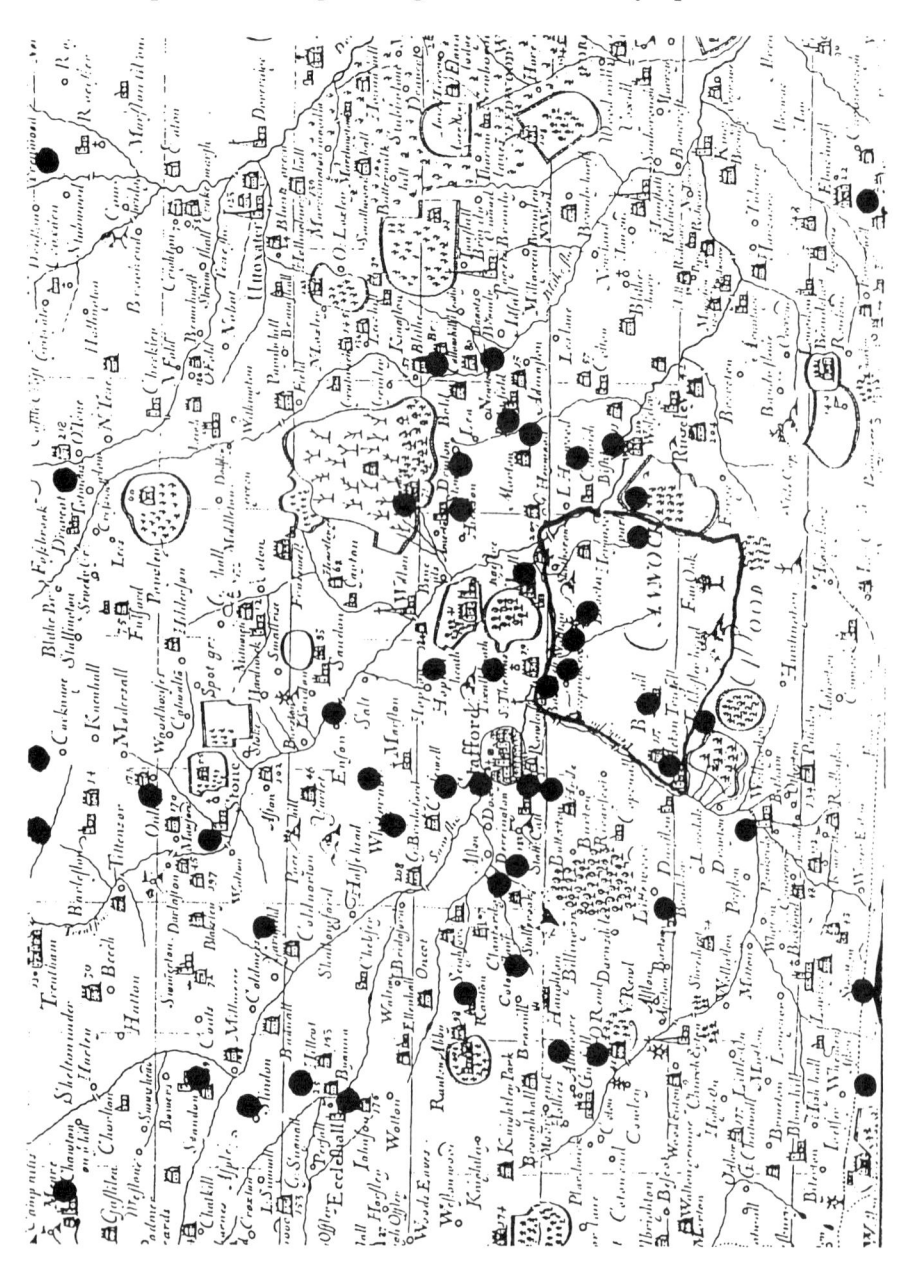

It was around the same time that Gerardus de Stafford gave up his effort to build the Priory. From records, it seems that the first building was demolished, and Bishop Richard Peche had the project started again around 1180. He dedicated it to St.Thomas the Martyr. Just how long it took to build the Priory we do not know, but progress must have been made within the first two years as, in 1182, Richard Peche had become a very tired man, having been sent by the King to Ireland to try to persuade them to accept the authority of the Pope, and to overcome the troubles which had arisen there. He gave up his See and took the habit of a "regular" Canon in the Priory, and was buried there in front of the altar of the church in the same year.

Let us look at the endowments which the Priory received from the Bishop and subsequent Bishops. (See early layout of the site on which the Priory was built - Map 2 on Page 44) For the foundation, Gerardus's original gift was about 70 acres of land, on the north side of the river Sow, called "Sheepwash Meadow", and as much of the river Sow as belonged to it. When Bishop Peche took over the project he gave to the Canons the whole river Sow, for fishing, from Stafford to "Water Wending" (which was on the opposite bank of the Sow from the Priory), and a place called "Le Kocholme", which was the marshy ground where the Penk joins the Sow. Later he gave them land called "Estmora", which was the area between the rivers-junction and westwards towards Baswich Church. As Richard Peche died in 1182, these further gifts must have been from Gerard Puella or Hugh de Nonant who followed him. By this time the canons had acquired the rights to fish the River Penk and had been allowed to construct fish ponds on the River Sow and the Kingston Brook, As the Kingston Brook was not within the rights of the Bishop, permission was needed from the local landowner. He also gave them permission to erect a Fulling Mill next to the fish pond - the remains of these are visible today. [Further reference to "the Bishop", through the years ahead, will mean the Bishop occupying the See at that time.]

By 1194 the Priory had received gifts of land at Acton Trussell and Bednall, Walton, Stockton, and Brocton, and gifts of land from manorial Lords far and wide not only in Staffordshire but from elsewhere in the Midlands. There was land at Tixall, Hopton, Rickerscote, Chartley and Gnosall. The list of their holding of land is so large that to fully realise the extent, we need to look at Map 3 on the opposite page - each ● represents a gift of land to the Priory. A good deal of the land given was poor, but the monks taught people how to reclaim land.

The Bishop in the early days of the Priory, did not have a Manor House at Baswich, his nearest being at Eccleshall, and he used the monks to reclaim a meadow at Eccleshall Manor in return for land adjoining, which he had given to them. They did however have their problems nearer home. The land in Sheepwash Meadow, being beside the river, regularly had its crops ruined when the river overflowed.

It does seem from the aforementioned list of gifts, that the Church and the surrounding manorial Lords had treated them most generously. Well, that was only half the blessing they received. The Crown gave them wood for building from Cank Forest, and a cartload of dead wood every week for burning. As happened with Baswich Church there were several churches, within Staffordshire and beyond, which were appropriated to the Priory. A regular income was received from tithes on land in the parish and beyond, plus gifts of gold and silver. After many years they were so rich that besides receiving land, they could afford to go out and buy land and property. In 1335 the Crown gave them, under licence, permission to acquire property worth £10 a year, which was only the beginning, for such grants were given year after year.

It would appear that some of the benefactors wanted something in return About 1200, when Walter de Grey gave the Priory a detached portion of Colwich parish, it was given on the condition that they receive him and his three children, whenever asked, and keep them in food and clothing. In 1258 Phillip de Mutton (Bradley & Gnosall) gave the Priory estates there, and when he died his son asked for the right to present a Canon who was to celebrate Mass for the soul of his father. The Crown also tried this "give and take" policy. In 1316 the Priory was asked to receive a William Deuros, an infirm royal servant, and to feed and clothe him during his lifetime. Two years later they tried the same with a William le Ferrour. It seems the Bishop thought he should try his luck, for he asked them to grant a pension of 40s to his barber, but the Archbishop was having none of this and castigated the Bishop, saying he thought such use of monastic revenues as sacrilegious.

So far we have had a look at the endowments, but what do we know about the building which was started in 1180. Records tell us very little. We can surmise that part of the church was completed by 1245, as Henry III gave the Canons £10 to buy a chasuble of red samite with orphreys, and in 1255 he gave them six timber oaks from the forest at Teddesley Hay, and, in 1272, ten oaks from Kinver forest. In 1275 Edward I gave the Canons 10 timber oaks for the roof of their church, and in 1290 another 6 for the same purpose. So it seems that the church was not completed until nearing the end of the 13th century.

To get some idea of what the completed Priory looked like we can only go on the findings of a Mr. Lynam, an authority on archaeology, and a member of the North Staffordshire Field Club, who, after his survey in 1878, drew the plan which when incorporated with another survey which was done at the Dissolution gives a general outline of the Priory (Map 2). It is only by building imaginary walls from the information we have, that it is possible to get some idea what the Priory looked like. (See plate 27 for an artist's impression) Apparently, from the Dissolution Survey in 1538, the Church is described as a wonderful building with four bells and a clock . It also mentions the Water

Chamber, the Great Chamber, two inner chambers, a chamber over the Chapel, and a carter's chamber, which was on the left of the main entrance. All were in the western range.

The Prior's Parlour was in the western range, behind the Grand Hall. The present farmhouse is over the site of the Prior's Parlour (Plates 30 & 31). The Grand Hall, in some reports, was taken to be the reception for visitors, but it could have been the Guest House where visitors were accommodated. All of these rooms had beds, and some reports mention silk drapes, far different from the life outside, where the poor slept on the floor.

In about 1960, I photographed the remaining parts, which have since become more overgrown, and posted the photographs to the Rev. J.C. Dickenson, an authority on British Monasteries. and he advised me of where he thought they fitted into the Priory layout. The details have been marked on Mr. Lynam's plan (Map 2). Not mentioned in the report are the two mills belonging to the Priory, which the Canons were given the right to erect in the early years. The first one was on the south-west corner, near the bridge over the mill stream, and was used as a corn mill. The second mill, which was a fulling mill, was on the Kingston Brook, north-west of the Priory. (See Map 1) As this was not in the Bishop's manor it was erected by permission of a local land owner.

Plate 30 Entrance Door to Parlour

Plate 31 Priors Parlour

The following is Rev. Dickenson's Report.

"There is no doubt that many of the present buildings of St.Thomas' stand on medieval sites. Such is certainly the case with the bridge (Plate 32) which retains a little medieval work, also the mill, the outbuilding near it on the other side of the stream and the present house. How much more of the medieval building survived the Dissolution to be destroyed in later times is not known, but it is possible that much of the north transept and of the southern range, with part of the western range and possibly the gate-house belonged to this category.

It is almost certain that the present entrance to the Priory is on the exact site of the medieval one. The practical convenience of this are obvious and the present entrance faces the west front of the church, as the medieval one would have done. Unfortunately we have no reference to the post Dissolution history of the gatehouse or any picture of it. It is unmentioned in the Dissolution survey and the same is true of the subsidiary building which stood near it. The long building near the stream has a little original work including the semi-circular headed door, perhaps of about 1500, and a small window in its western gable which may well belong to the same period. (Possibly the buttery, bakehouse, and the cookhouse). Its eastern end may contain older work. The long building parallel to it which stands between it and the road has no such medieval details.

Plate 32 St Thomas' Mill Bridge

Of the principal buildings of the monastery only three have left any trace - the conventual church and the western and southern ranges of the cloister court - and none of these is at all imposing in its present condition.

THE CONVENTUAL CHURCH.
The only part of this now visible is a stretch of walling some 39 feet long - part of the bank which bounds the northern side of the garden. (Plate 33)

Plate 33 North Wall of Priory Church

Comparison of the present walling with a scaled drawing of it in the William Salt Library shows a little deterioration in its condition since 1877. (Plate 34) The two main features are a respond which stands to full height with its original capital and, immediately to the east of it, a plain aumbry. There is no doubt that this work belongs to the first half of the 13th century or that it is the remains of the north wall of the north transept of the church. The respond supported an arch leading into an eastern chapel to which the aumbry pertained. It is not impossible that all or part of the north transept was retained as a domestic chapel at the Dissolution, but this is pure surmise. The Dissolution survey mentions "cross yeles" (ie transepts) but tells us nothing else which adds to our knowledge of the plan of the church. The only chapel which is mentioned is the Lady Chapel, though there must have been several more. Excavation of the ground plan of the church would probably be a fairly easy matter as the site is unencumbered and the

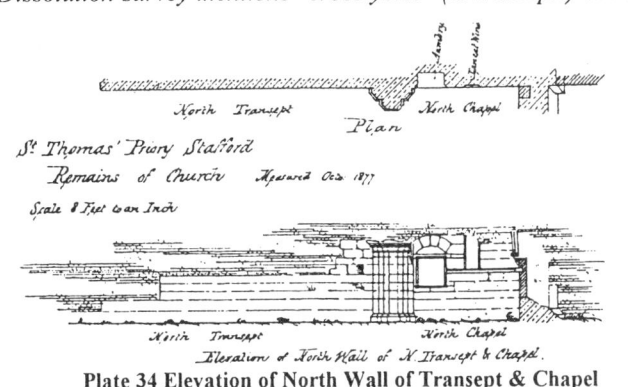

Plate 34 Elevation of North Wall of Transept & Chapel

Ancient Parish of Berkswich.

original level not far below the present one, whilst the remaining walling of the north wall of the north transept makes the location of the crossing and south transept an easy matter (Plate 35). The original west end of the church has gone but may have been in line with the west wall of the house. It is not known whether the nave had one or two aisles, or none at all. Comparison with similar sites suggest it is quite likely to have a northern aisle but not a southern one. At the north east angle of the house is a rough projecting piece of masonry of uncertain purpose which may be medieval"

Plate 35 North Wall of North Transept running across top of Photo.

We have looked at the endowments of the Priory and the possible layout of the buildings, so now let us have a look at the Canons and note their functions. The head or chief office at the Priory was the Prior, next would come the sub-Prior, and the usual order, according to the number of offices, would be the Precentor, the Succentor, the Sacrist, the Cellerar, the Grainger, the Receiver, the Fraterer, the Kitchener, the Chamberlain, the Hosteller, the Master of the Farmery, and the Almoner. Each is responsible for some part of the management of the Priory.

Let us imagine we could join them to see their daily routine. A little bell (nola) summoned the Canons and roused them from their sleep for Matins, (the first service of the day). The primary work of the Canons consisted of service in the church. This was the work of God (Opus Dei) which, in fact, took up the largest part of the day. These services were the seven hours and celebrations, (1) Matins, i.e., Nocturns and Lauds sung at midnight, (2) Prime, sung at daybreak in the morning celebration (missa matutinalis) and this in turn was followed by the chapter. We enter the church both at midnight and prime, and listen to the Canons' devotions. This ended, we follow them into the chapter house, for here, day by day, the business of the whole house is transacted. At the close of chapter (3) Tierce is sung in church about 9 am., and is followed by the High Celebration and (4) Sext, which is at midday. During the day and between the services a certain time is set apart for reading, writing, and illuminating manuscripts, for which the cloister is used, and we can walk around and see them silently at work. Dinner is served in the frater (or refectory). As silence is the rule there is reading during the meal, each Canon taking the office of Reader in turn, week by week. The Canons could then return to the cloister or to the dorter (or dormitory) until (5) nones about 3 p.m. (6) Evensong was followed by supper. Then came collation, and, after collation, (7) compline. After this all Canons return to the dorter and "felles" or, in later days, to the various "chambers". This is the way each day was observed at the Priory.

If we go into the Chapter House and see what happens there we notice that, in accordance with the "Rule", when all had taken their seats, one of the brethren went to the pulpit and read a selection from the martyrology of the day. Then the priest of the week read the psalms and collects, which were followed by the appointed portion of the "Rule". Then brief notices of the day were given out, and the duties of those responsible, both in the church and outside, were read out. A sermon was then preached, after which all strangers had to leave.

In the frater, where the meals were served, there was a table set cross-ways at one end of the hall, at which sat the prelate and any guest who happened to be staying at the Priory, and at the other tables, which ran down the length of the hall, sat the Canons who had their backs to the wall. Usually there were three courses, meat or fish, eggs and salt fish, vegetables and fruit, but the staple food was always bread, laid upon the tables before the Canons came in. On entering, each Canon brought with him a knife; the spoon was already in place for him. Had we been attending this meal on Passion Sunday, 1280, we would have seen the Archbishop of Canterbury, John Peckham, there, and if we had visited the "great chamber" we would have seen that, when everyone else was in bed, the Archbishop was busy writing a letter to the King (Edward I) complaining that he had been refused admission to a certain church in Stafford called St. Mary's, and that this was apparently by order of the King. He was complaining that he could not hold a visitation to St. Mary's or any other dependant chapels, because it was a Royal Free Church. Furthermore, he was aggrieved that on the King's order, entry was to be resisted by force, including the use of armed men. He went on to say he would defer from demanding visitations there until he had spoken to his Majesty. It seems that the Archbishop did not get the result he wanted, for the King insisted on upholding, against all Archbishops and Bishops, the liberties of the Mercian Royal Free Chapels. There must have been something at the Priory which the Archbishop liked, for, the following year, he granted the church of Audlem to the Priory, which church, on his visit to the Priory in 1280, he had found to be empty.

When Bishop Burghill gave the advowson of Baswich Church to the Priory, he stated at the time that the Priory was poverty-stricken and burdened with much alms-giving, being situated on the road to Stafford. It is understandable that it was described as "offering hospitality to travellers", and it was common to most Priories to have a guest-house, or similar buildings, where they would offer two-night accommodation to visitors. One of the most famous visitors was Henry IV when he stopped there after his victory at the Battle of Shrewsbury in 1403. The monks were credited with the sum of 26s 8d for two-days entertainment. The cultivated palate of Henry did not find much to suite his taste in the well-stocked wine cellar of the Priory. It is said that he sent for three pipes of Gascon wine from the royal cellars. (This would be equivalent to about 2000 modern bottles of wine)

When one looks at the recorded spiritual life of the Canons, there is bound to be the question of *"what else did they do?"* In 1191, just after this Priory was founded, Peter de Bois, who was dean of St. Peter's in Wolverhampton, criticised the Canons, who served many of the collegiate churches in Staffordshire, because of their of low standards. He persuaded King John and the Archbishop of Canterbury to replace the Canons with monks, and even wrote to the Pope about their evil and satanic ways. Had some similar trait been found by Bishop Northburgh when he visited the Priory in 1347? He found that the frequent absence of the sub-Prior on business had led to a breakdown of regular discipline and had encouraged waste and needless expense. No accounts and no inventory of the Priory's goods were available. Three of the Canons kept hounds in the Priory and went hunting with a company of laymen. Some Canons considered themselves better-born than their brethren, and had adopted worldly fashions in their dress, going about in tunics and peaked boots, with knives in their belts. The Bishop forbade the Prior to employ the sub-Prior on business outside the Priory, and ordered that annual accounts were to be kept by the obedienteries, and by any Canon who was given charge of the Priory's goods. In future no Canon was to hunt or keep hounds or hawks, and all were to adopt the regular dress. Canon wishing to visit family or friends would only be allowed to do so once a year, for eight days, and then only if accompanied by one of his brethren. The Bishop also ordered than his visitation decrees were to be read in chapter four times a year. It seems that this was too much for the Prior as he resigned later that same year.

It seems that things did not change much over the years and one wonders why. Judging from the records of gifts received, income from property, including houses and shops, returns from the lands, which the Priory now owned and farmed, it appears that in 1518 (coming up to the Dissolution) the Priory was £49 in debt, but was owed £100.

The Prior claimed that there had been an income of £140 for the year, which was 20 marks better than the previous year. The sub-Prior thought the Prior ruled the house autocratically, but well, although I doubt if Bishop Blythe agreed when he visited the Priory in 1524. The same slackness was very much in evidence.

The Bishop ordered that the Prior should render his accounts before the whole convent. He should take a new inventory of the Priory's goods, He should take the advice of his brethren only, and not that of laymen; and he should secure payment of the debts owed to the Priory, if necessary by the process of law. Also some brethren still did not sleep in the dormitory, the complaints about the neglect of the refectory were repeated, some of the servants were alleged to be dishonest, and the Prior did not render an account or keep an inventory.

Plate 36 Henry VIII & Seal

Away from the Priory other events were taking place, which were to greatly affect the future. Henry VIII (Plate 36) had fallen in love with Ann Boleyn, a maid of honour at Court, and he wanted to marry her. He instructed Archbishop Wolsey to begin talks with the Pope for a divorce. When the Pope could not agree, Henry blamed Wolsey, whom he sacked, and appointed, in his place, Thomas Cranmer. Cranmer meekly pronounced the marriage to Catherine at an end. He did not perform the marriage between the King and Ann Boleyn; this was performed by his chaplain, Rowland Lee. The King reward Lee by appointing him Bishop of Coventry and Lichfield. The Pope declared the marriage illegal, and Henry replied by renouncing the supremacy of the Pope, and declared himself head of the English Church. Along with all the other problems this created, he was concerned about the low state of his treasury. To fill it again he resorted to a disgraceful act. He ordered that, first the smaller monasteries and then the larger ones, should be dissolved, and the incomes, rents and capital should be paid into the royal exchequer. The Crown commissioners, in sacking the monasteries, were a ruthless bunch. It appears that their main interest was in stripping away the lead, which most of the buildings had in abundance, and melting it into ingots. The buildings were reduced to a level which made them uninhabitable. There are no records to show what the effect was at St.Thomas', which the Priors, it seems, had managed to hold on to by bribing Cromwell.

In 1535, just prior to the Dissolution, an inventory was taken in preparation for the sale of the Priory contents. The accounts of the Priory showed the gross annual value of the Priory's possessions as £180 18s 9d, a figure which made it the wealthiest house of the Order in the county. Gross temporal income amounted to £130 16s 5d. (net.£115 12s 6d.) and gross spiritual income, after deductions, came to £26 0s 7d. Total net income was £141 13s 2d., almost exactly the figure given by the Prior in 1518. Some reports say that when the dissolution seemed imminent in 1536, the Bishop (Rowland Lee) was casting a covetous eye over the Priory and its estates. It seems he was not alone, as interest in the Priory had been shown by Lord Stafford and other manorial lords. The Prior also had an interest in getting exemption from the suppression order, but it seemed that he wasted his money in trying to bribe Cromwell.

But, before we come to the dissolution when the life of this Priory would be changed irretrievably, let us give a thought to the monks who did so much to change the land and erect the buildings. There is no mention of them in the reports, although we learn of them in the reclamation of land and the erection of buildings and, true to their tradition, they must have done untold good for the poor of the parish. The numbers in 1536 were 6 Canons and 29 monks, which were below the strength of earlier years.

Without doubt, at this time, all the people in the Priory were wondering what was going to happen, so did the Prior and so did the Bishop (Rowland Lee.). It seems it was the Bishop who made the first move, for, early in 1536, he tried to bribe Cromwell. In asking that he should press his case with the King, he suggested that there would be money for the King's Highness and a certain sum for himself. Just in case the Archbishop did not want to play, he put forward his point of view that, as the land of the Priory came from the Church, he hoped he might have preference of the house and land for" one of his kinsfolk". (He rather rephrased that in a subsequent attempt). This action has been condemned, since, in histories of the Priory. As the Priory and its extensive endowments of land, both in, and outside, the parish belonged to the Church, they should not have been granted elsewhere without safeguards.

By June of the same year he had obtained assurances that he would get the Priory, whilst at the same time the Prior was paying Cromwell to use his influence on the Prior's behalf. Some reports say Ann Boleyn pressured the King on the Bishop's behalf in return for his services in performing their marriage ceremony. In the next month the Priory was exempted from suppression under the Act, which dissolved the lesser monasteries, no doubt as a result of the £133 6s 8d, which the Canons had promised the Crown for toleration and continuance. As it turned out this was more than the Prior could pay, being almost a year's income. He sent Cromwell two amounts, one of £60 and one of £20, and asked for time to pay a further £20. Knowing of this the Bishop again made a further request for the Priory, accusing the Prior of unreasonable waste. He said he wanted the Priory at an easy rent, so that his "poor" nephews might have some relief thereby. (It was said that, at this time, the Bishop was the most active agent of the King in the suppression of the monasteries, but later he converted to the Popish Party.) The poor nephews, to whom the Bishop referred were sons of his sister Isabel and her husband Roger Fowler of Broomhill, Norfolk, (part of the family of the later Dukes of Norfolk), descended from an ancient Buckinghamshire family. Their parents died early, and the Bishop took charge of them.

The last plea of the Bishop had the desired effect for, later in 1538, Prior Whytell and 5 Canons surrendered the Priory and all its possessions to the Crown. The Canons who signed the surrender were Richard Harvey (sub-Prior), Xtopher Simson, Thomas Bageley, Brother Wm. Pykestock, Brother Wm. Stapulton, and Brother Wm. Bordon. The Prior received a pension of £26.13s 4d, and the 5 Canons pensions ranging from £6 to £5. The 29 monks received gratuities. On the day following the surrender, (although the Bishop did not get the grant of the Priory and all its lands until the following year), the contents of the Priory were put up for sale. It seems that he stepped in to purchase part of the fabric of the Priory Church, the cloister and the chapter house, the furnishing and fittings of the Priory, timber, hay and farm instruments plus cattle at Baswich and Orberton, all for £87. Plate weighing 28oz remained unsold, whilst other plate had been mortgaged for £43 by the Prior. Lead worth £40, four bells from the church worth £54, and the fabric of other buildings within the precinct remained unsold. (The unsold silver plate remained a mystery for many years.) Whilst there are no records, extant, indicating the "sacking" of the Priory by the Crown Commissioners, this would seem to be what took place in 1538.

In 1539 the Priory and all its lands were granted to Bishop Rowland Lee, and when he died four years later, on January 24th 1543, the land and most of the property passed to his sister's second son, named Bryan Fowler. He, and his descendants managed to continue at the Priory for the next 200 years with a centre for the Catholic faith.

The other sons inherited other lands and properties in other parts of Staffordshire, and beyond, which had belonged to the Priory. Without doubt the making of some rich families.

In 1564 Bishop Bentham complained that Bryan was harbouring the ex-Bishop of Peterborough at the Priory, and that, as a result, "divers lewd priests have resort thither". Bryan married Jane, daughter and heiress of John Hanmer of Bettsfield, Flintshire, and ultimately Bryan came into possession of that estate.

Bryan was summoned before the Council as a papist in 1575, 1576, 1580 and 1581. He was succeeded in 1587 by Bryan and Jane's eldest son, Walter, who, on the death of his father, took over the Priory, which at that time was renamed St.Thomas's Hall.

Walter Fowler died in 1621. One of Walter's sons, William, became a Dominican priest and served as chaplain at St.Thomas', and, on his death, he was buried there.

The Civil War brought great trouble to the Fowlers on account of their recusancy, and one would expect that they were affected by the Battle of Hopton Heath in 1643, which took place almost on their doorsteps.

But life at the Priory went on for the Fowlers, Walter had a son also called Bryan, who died in 1658, he had a son Walter, who died in 1683, who in turn had a son Walter, who married Constantia, the daughter of Walter, first Lord Aston of Tixall.

At about this time, 1684-1688, another inventory of the Priory was made (See Appendix), while the last of the "Walters" was there. He died in 1695 and bequeathed the Priory and all its lands to his brother, William, who died in 1717 without a male heir. It seems that this last inventory attracted the attention of the apostate Richard Hitchmore, who for a time had been chaplain to Bishop Witham. Apparently he noticed something

Plate 37 Pillaton Chalice & Plate

was missing, and, in a letter to the Forfeited Estates Commission, he informed them of valuable chalices and other altar-silver, formerly seen and used by him when officiating as a priest.

He detailed one large silver chalice, one paten (one other silver chalice and paten, double-gilt with gold), two large silver crucibles, one large silver plate for the said crucibles to stand upon, two large silver thuribles, six large silver candlesticks, and a large silver crucifix carried in procession on Maundy Thursday, and a large silver ciborium, double- gilt within with gold, in which was kept the consecrated Host. There is no report of the Commission obtaining any of the missing items, but the chalice and paten, (Plate 37), turned up some time later, in 1794, during the demolition of Pillaton Hall, the home of the Littletons. It was identified as almost certainly once belonging to the Priory. On the base of the chalice was the black-letter inscription "*Pater de celis deus misereri nobis*", and on the paten "*Sancta trinitas unus deus misereri noblis*"

Walter was the last of the Fowlers and the estate passed to John Betham, who was husband of William's niece, Kath Casey. John Betham died in 1719, and the estate passed to his daughter Catherine, aged 9 at that time. In 1726 she married Thomas Belasyse, (Viscount Fauconberg), who took possession of the Priory.

At this point, the start of a legal battle was in the making. William had left two wills, one dated 1712, and one 1715, and the latter had been suppressed. In the latter will he also made a bequest to his sister who had married a John Grove of Worcester, and this bequest, in turn, passed on to their daughter, Rebecca Grove. When the second will came to light it was laid before Mr. Richard Fitzgerald, an Irish barrister, for his opinion. I suppose he, seeing a chance to get part of the Fowler estate, married Rebecca. Letters of Administration for the will were granted in 1729, and as Lord Fauconberg disputed the will, there was a long and costly suit in Chancery, followed by an appeal to the House of Lords. The result was that Fauconberg had to surrender part of the estate to the Irish barrister, Fitzgerald. He retained the Priory, but in disgust Fauconberg hastily sold the Priory of St. Thomas to the notorious Sarah, Duchess of Marlborough. There were further protests at this time that the Priory and all its lands should have been returned to the church, but , as Lord Fauconberg conformed to the Church of England, all the funds and goods, held in trust by the Fowler family for the clergy, were lost to the Catholic Church. The Duchess, who died in 1744, left it all to her grandson, the Hon. John Spencer, fourth son of Charles, Earl of Sunderland. In 1765 the Hon. John Spencer was created Earl Spencer. He sold the estate to Lord Talbot, who, in turn, left it to the Shrewsburys.

A firm of cotton spinners took over the Priory when the Fowlers died out in the early 1700s but they only stayed a few years. It is thought that they were responsible for adding brick to the medieval stonework in many of the buildings. It is thought that at this time the stone pillars, which formed the entrance to the Chapter House, were sold off to the Chetwynds to be used in the building of Brocton Hall. At the same time the outer wall was reduced in height, and the gatehouse was demolished. The stonework from the gateway could have been bought by the Levetts for it is said that the stone which forms part of an gateway to the gardens of Milford Hall came from St Thomas' Priory.

Whilst there, the cotton spinners gave employment to both adults and children to the extent that a report in 1750 mentioned that "the town of Stafford is greatly increased of late in numbers and wealth by their manufacture of cloth". When they left, the Mill was used for a Corn-milling business which carried on until the beginning of the 20th century (Plate 38). When the cotton spinners left the buildings were again converted to form two farms, Priory Farm and Mill Farm.

Plate 38 Mill circa 1910

As our visit to the Priory of St.Thomas the Martyr comes to an end we must not forget the legend that surrounds the Priory. It was said that in medieval times, a young local girl was chased into the Priory and murdered, and there can still be heard the sound of the crying of a young girl.

As we leave the Priory and scan the remains of the centre of early Christian activity, one cannot help but feel a consciousness of the remains of Bishop Peche, Bishop of Coventry and Lichfield, Robert de Ferrers, 8th Earl of Derby, Bryan Fowler and his wife and all the monks, who were buried in the cemetery at the rear of the church, some of whose graves were disturbed when some heifers were buried by the farmer at the beginning of this century. Plate 39 shows a stone coffin, and, beside it, the remains of a monk, who was buried without a coffin. It has also been said that the remains of monks lie buried without coffins near the Mill Farm.

Plate 39 Stone Coffin & Skeleton

It seems that farming has almost come to an end at both farms, so should not the area be declared a Christian burial ground, and what could be more fitting than for it to be converted into a tourist-site, where one could sit in the solitude of this part of the parish and enjoy the beauties of nature?

As we leave the Priory to continue our journey to Stockton, we retrace our steps along Baswich Lane. Plate 40 shows how the approach to the church looked at the turn of the century.

Just after we have passed the church there is a lane on the left, now named Baswich Crest. This was the only turning off Baswich Lane until the houses came. If you look back at Map 1 on page 13, you will see the start of a footpath, which goes right across Stockton Common and into the hamlet of Stockton. This was the path, which was trodden each Sunday by the Levett family and their staff, going from Milford Hall to church at Baswich.

Plate 40 Baswich Church c1900

Ancient Parish of Berkswich.

Map 4 : Walton 1734 - 1850

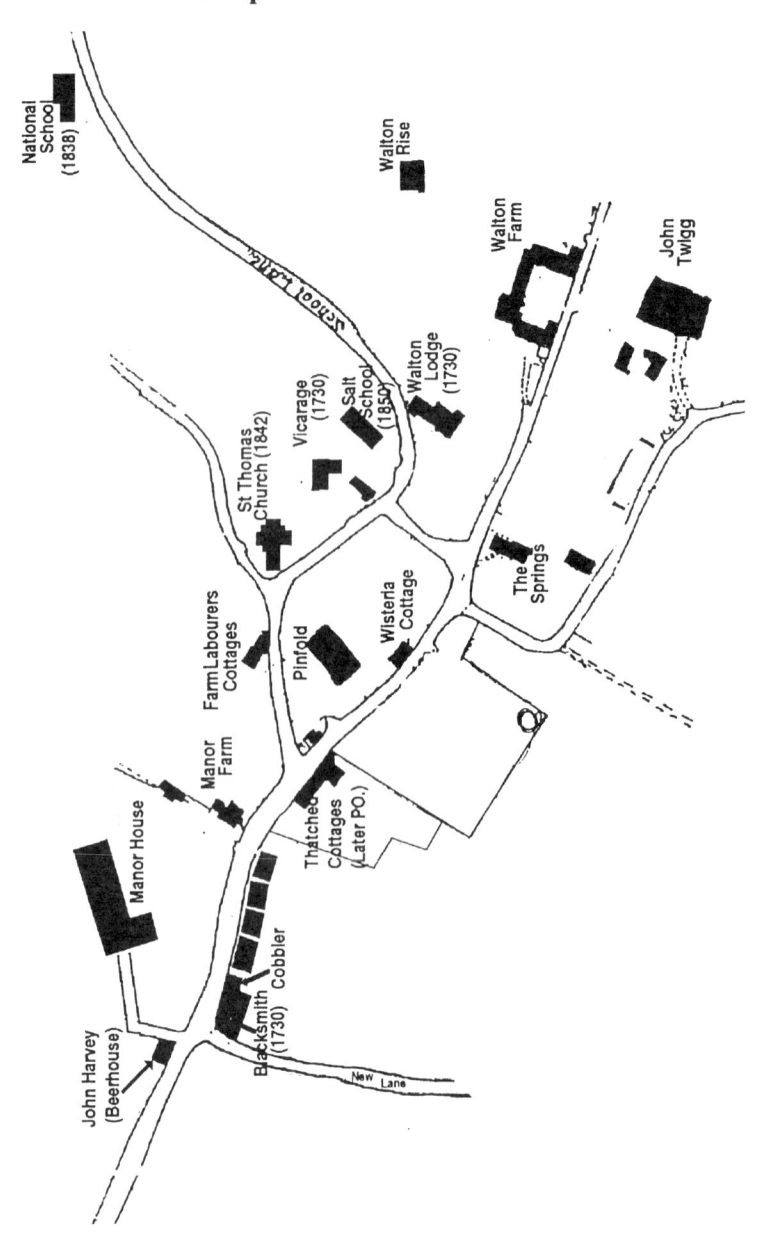

Chapter 6
STOCKTON & WALTON
(Part 1. 1650 to 1850)

The part of the story on Stockton and Walton, I have split into two chapters, 1650 to 1850, and then 1851 to 1921. In the first part there is what one might call the "coming to life" of the area, and, in the second, is the development-period of the area.

Had we left the Priory in early 1700 when it was sold and followed the road back towards Baswich, there would only be the River Sow to cross until 1766, when the canal was constructed. It was to be another 80 years before the railway was built parallel to the waterways. (See Map 1).

Until the 20th century Stockton was a small hamlet with only five or six cottages. East of the hamlet is Stockton Common, and beyond that is Townhills, which can only be reached by a footpath crossing.

Plate 42 Waterman's Canal Bank Cottages

To reach the far side of the canal, one had to go under the railway bridge and over the canal bridge where there was a solitary house, which could only have been for a waterway man. It was built towards the end of the 18th century, soon after the canal was built, to house the Tollman. Barges had to stop at the Toll-House and the Tollman would come out with a pole, which he would put into the water at the side of the barge and he could tell, by the difference in depth of the water to its normal depth, what the displacement weight of the barge was. From this he could calculate the load being carried, and would charge the appropriate toll. (Plate 42).

Let us revert in our story to before the canal and the railway came, and look at the early history of Stockton.

We find it was called "Stoken" in 1284, "St.Thomas Stokken" in 1314, "Stokton-juxta-le Cannok" in 1360, and "Banco Stoketon" in 1544. Also about this time it was recorded as *"the place which had a farmstead belonging to the religious place, near St.Thomas' Priory"*. It could therefore be that there was a farm run by the monks, the location of which we have no trace. The earliest record of people living in Stockton is on a Muster Roll in the time of Henry VIII. According to it, the Twiggs appear to be in Stockton, as well as Walton, in the 16th century. We do not know if they were just working the land for, at this period, the land belonged to the Bishop. There are no records available to show just when they owned land in Stockton and Walton, but the Twiggs have on record that they were *"yeoman-holders and cultivators of their own land, very pure of extraction, and ancient in possession of their soil"*.

The earliest record of landowners in Stockton after the Fowlers, and the battle in the courts between Fauconbergs and Fitzgeralds, was of course the notorious Sarah, Duchess of Marlborough. Records show that her land descended to the Shrewsburys via the Talbots in the second half of the 18th century. It would, therefore, seem that there were other owners of land in Stockton, in addition to the land which had belonged to the Priory, for records show that, in 1650, land was sold to William Farmer, described as at *"Nockings, in the parish of Bassage"* with a right to common pastures and also a right to dig turves on a common in Cannock Forest. In 1667 Farmer's daughter, Ellen, married Edward Byrd, son of Anthony Byrd, (who had property in St. Mary's Passage, Stafford), and who, from the late 17th century, had been acquiring land and property far and wide. On the death of William Farmer his land also passed to the Byrds, and then in 1771, on the death of John Byrd, without male issue, his eldest daughter Lucy inherited. She married the Rev. Richard Levett of High Wycombe. So from the late 18th century the two principal Stockton landowners seem to have been the Levetts and the Shrewsburys.

Having seen the route through which land ownership came to Stockton after the time of the Priory, our main interest is in who lived there.

The earliest records to give us some clue to this are the Parish Charities. As there were no such things as postal districts in those days, we have names without addresses. There were six poor people at Stockton and Townhills receiving charity, and the names of two benefactors living there. In 1717, John Twigg and Richard Watwood were men who helped to mould the future of the parish. Records show that the cottage, in which John Twigg lived, was surrendered to him by William Farmer, (mentioned above.) This would seem to be the same John Twigg who is shown living at Barnfields in 1745. It was the sons of Richard Twigg from Walton, John and Samuel, who built Weeping Cross House.

As far as I know, there are no records which show precisely where either man lived in Stockton. What we do know is that, about 1800, a John Twigg built Stockton Farm (Plate 43) on land which by then would be owned by the Levett family. It is assumed that this would be the same farm building which stood until the 1950's. It was a very roomy farm house with oak beams, and an inglenook fireplace in the dining room. It stood in a lovely garden and there was a large malthouse with a malt kiln and a special floor for drying the grain. In 1850 the tenant farmer was a man called Jno Kingstone, and in Stockton at the same time was a shoemaker with the same name. The further development of Stockton is included with Walton in the next Chapter.

Plate 43 Stockton Farm

As we leave Stockton Farm we are, within a short distance, on the main road to Lichfield, described as being a rutted rough road when the stage-coaches started to run about 1785. The Holyhead Coach passed through Milford and Walton on its way to

Stafford. The mail coaches were exempt from toll. They carried guards armed with blunderbusses and two pistols. Prior to this, in 1677, there were six post-routes in the country, and the Holyhead route passed through Stone, Stafford and Lichfield. Post-boys riding the pack-horses travelled between towns. It was the responsibility of the people living alongside the road to carry out the maintenance, but generally the burden became so great that, in 1663, an Act of Parliament set up the system of turnpike-trusts to pay for repairs to the roads, but the road through Walton was never turnpiked. It was only turnpiked from Haywood (Shugborough) southwards about a hundred years later.

It will be seen by reference to Map 4, on Page 62, that, in this early period, the main road to Lichfield ran through Walton Village as there was no bypass until 1850. Stage-coaches had to climb Walton Bank, (later called "The Rise"). to the village, which, in 1068, was described in the Domesday Book as a hamlet of four cottages and four acres of meadow. It was said to be set in a clearing of Cannock Forest, which still ran down to the bank of the river at Radford.

Before that, in the early Anglo-Saxon days, an appraisal of this district described it as follows:- "*The English who founded Stafford as a site for a town, penned the local Britons in Walton at a safe distance away, and here the displaced Britons were allowed to live as a community.*"

Back in the reign of Henry VIII, so the records say, the Commissioners, Lord Stafford, Thomas Gifford, Edward Lyttleton and Edward Aston, called a Muster Roll of all able men over 16 in Stockton and Walton. They declared that the following men were able and had harness:-

Ralf Madden	had a gestern,
William Blythe	a bow, a sheaf of arrows and a bill.
John Sharpe had harness for a man.	
Henry Twigg	had the same
Richard Twigg	had the same.
Harry Malle had a bill.	
Thomas Harding	had a bill and a pair of splentes.
Hugh Baggeley	)
William Twigg	) all had horses, gesterns and a pair of splentes each.
Harry Twigg	)
Hugh Wythnell	) had a gestern and a sallett
Ralph Mynors	)
John Bagley	) had a pair of Briggidyrons, splentes, a bill and a sallett.

"Splentes"	were armour, or plates, worn on arms or legs.
"Briggidyrons"	were either irons set over the fire to support pots or pans, or else irons used in spanning a river in bridge-building.
"Bill"	was a battle axe.
"Harness"	was leather armour.
"Sallett"	was a helmet or head piece.
"Gestern"	was a coat of mail.

In 1575 one Richard Lees of Walton died. He was buried in Holy Trinity, Berkeswich. In his will he left 4d. to each God-child; to his manservant Thomas Ward, he left a lamb, and to his maid servant, Alice Aleyn, he left 6d.

In 1577 one John Geffrey, of Walton, in the Parish of Baswich, died, and was buried in a "Christen buryall". Amongst his bequests was one of 12d. and a pair of shoes, to an old woman called "Mother Barbour". To the Parson he left one yoke and gearing.

In 1599 at Michaelmas, Sara Lees, Kathleen Glover, Joan Hardern, Anne Mynors and Helen Hurlesdon, broke into the house of Henry Pinson, at Walton (he was a free agent of William Paget of Haywood Manor), and withheld possession from Henry. They were tried by the Earl of Essex and ordered to restore possession to Henry Pinson. Walter Wrottelsey was Sheriff at the time.

Moving on to the 18th century, the main road through the village of Walton, followed, as far as we know, the same route until the 19th Century. The church had not been built, and the area between what we now know as School Lane and the road where the village pump stands, was joined up by the short road returning to School Lane. This was the village green. However, whilst that could be a possibility, it does, to the present day, have a brick built enclosure known as "The Pinfold". In 1609 the address of Richard Twigg in the hamlet of Walton was "The Pinfold", but as previously mentioned, there was an absence of full addresses in the 17th century. One wonders if Richard Twigg built a house on what earlier had been the village green. What is certain is that the Twiggs became master-builders in the parish, and John the master-builder of a family. He fathered 12 children; Henry Twigg fathered 6. We know of Richard's son John living at "The Pinfold", and it is possible that Roger and his brother Samuel also lived there.

The Domesday Book of 1068 records four cottages at "Waltone" and, by the 17th century, it had grown very slowly. It would seem that the men with the money and the ability to develop the parish were attracted to building their homes at Walton because of its elevated position. Another attraction would be the main road to London passing through. As early as 1733 there was a blacksmith on the corner of New Lane, (which we now know as Old Croft Road.). His name was John Smith; next door was a cobbler named James Smith. As the stage-coaches started to pass through the village, as well as private coaches, there would be a growing trade for the blacksmith. The stage coach, the "Red Rocket", passed through for London at 2am., and the "Traveller" at 2pm. Mention was made in early records that there was a demand for an Inn to be built next door to the blacksmith, but it never materialised. It was not until 1800 that a "beerhouse" was built on the opposite corner. (There is still a shop there today, but the present one only dates from the 20th century.)

An early record written in pencil, which one can calculate was written in the early 20th century, tells us that the man, who kept the beerhouse, was a John Harvey, and that one day a man came out drunk. He fell, and hit his head on a stone which killed him. The incident was witnessed by John Keeling, who was 5 years old at the time and lived with his parents at "Wysteria Cottage". The report added :- *"The boy was very upset but his mother made him go to school the next day"*.

Plate 44 Manor House (West wing)

A few yards along the road, on the same side, was the entrance to what I believe was originally called the "Manor House". (Plate 44). It was a large house with 42 rooms, and lovely views from all of its windows, especially the east bedroom windows, which had a balcony overlooking the valley of the river towards Haywood and Tixall, with the Chase in the background. A stone wall ran along the main road at the front, with a long sweeping drive leading up to the house. There was an enclosed kitchen garden and orchard. At the side were stables for the horses. It was, at the start of the 20th century, renamed "Walton-on-the-Hill" by Lady Salt. The question is who lived there when it was built? My guess, going solely on dates, is that it could have been either Thomas Twist, who lived in Walton in 1689, or Edward Harding. who lived there about the time the Manor was built. Thomas Twist died in 1759, and whilst there is no record of when Edward Harding died, we do know that his son carried on in Walton after him. I therefore think it was Harding. - the Twiggs were further down the village.

The Hardings appeared to be mindful of the plight of the poorer people around them. It was a requirement of the Poor Law Act of 1601 and later Acts that each parish should be responsible for its own poor. Charities provided bread for the poor and issues of flannel in the winter. Some of the poor people would travel between parishes to see if they could fare better elsewhere than in their own parish. Ultimately they had to prove where they came from and the parish policeman had the task of "deporting" offenders. It appears that Michael Harding felt he should use his resources to help the poor. A minute in the report, of the 27th October 1801, of the meeting of the "Church Wardens and Overseers of the Poor", read :-   *"A meeting held this day at the house of Sam Copestick at Weeping Cross, it was resolved that a house should be opened for the reception of the poor of the parish of Baswich, and that the buildings offered by Mr. Michael Harding at the annual rent of six pounds six shillings for the above purpose, be engaged against Lady Day next".*

At the end of the year there was an item which said that Mr. Harding paid £10 for the thatching of the workhouse roof. There does not seem to be any trace of the site of the workhouse, or of the Stocks, which the same meeting decided should be built in the village.

Adjoining Manor House was Manor Farm, (later called Congreve House.), which was built about 1736. It was of wooden construction with plastering of wattle and daub. The interior had a wealth of oak, some of the beams being 18 inches thick. There was an oak staircase which led to the upper floors. The first farmer there was called Congreve. In 1742 he had a son named William, (later Sir William, Bart.), who entered the Army and became Superintendent of Military Machines. This William had a son also named William, who also became Sir William, the inventor of the Congreve Rocket.

Almost opposite the farm was a terrace of thatched cottages, which later became known as the Post Office.(Plate 45) They were built in the 17th century of ships' timbers, wattle and daub, which was later infilled with brick. It is not certain if there were two or three joined cottages, but different characteristics in doors and walls suggest three, although we only know of two people who lived in them. One was named Smith, and the other was Genners, a cobbler. Could it be that they were connected with the blacksmith and the cobbler on the corner ?.

Plate 45 Thatched Cottages, which later became 'The Post Office'

If we follow the Map of the village on page 62, and keep to the road on the right, it will take us past the village pump which in this period (1650 to1850) had a well at the side. As far as one can tell, from old records, it would be about 1850 that a Rev. Fuller drove his wife down the village to the well, and there, joined by a Mrs K. (could this have been the farmer's wife Mrs Kent, or even Mrs Keeling of Wysteria Cottage opposite ?), proceeded to jump down the well. A comment was made, *"It was cold at the bottom"*. The village pump not only supplied water for the villagers, it was the meeting point for a bit of village gossip.

Also appearing in the early records is the annual ceremony of "Perambulating the Boundaries", when choir and parishioners walked the bounds of the parish, stopping at ten Gospel Places to sing a psalm. The choirboys earned a small payment for each psalm sung. (The ceremony has recently been revived.)

Virtually opposite the village pump was "Wysteria Cottage" (Plate 46) The original with thatched roof could perhaps be dated by the old wall adjoining, but there is an early record, which tells us that Hales Keeling lived there in 1694. He appears to be the first of the Keelings; there followed Sampas and then John. Sampas was the first postmaster in the village, which would be in the mid-1800s. It is not known if he performed the duties of postmaster from Wysteria Cottage or from a cottage close by called " The Springs".

Plate 46 Wysteria Cottage (Left) Springs (Centre)

Post Office
"The Springs", as you will see from Plate 47 which was taken in 1899, was a Post Office, but it was built much earlier, on land which belonged to the Ansons (Lichfields), as indeed did all the land in this corner of the parish, until we reach the bounds of the Chetwynd and Levett estates. "The Springs" was small and damp, with a spring running at the side, hence its name.

Looking at Map 4, we reach the area between the footpath, which later ran past Walton Farm, (and on to Jacob's Ladder), and the road which goes to Brocton. At this time the "Bury" had not been built, but there are old foundations nearby, which suggest there may have been an earlier building before the "Bury". Perhaps one of the Twiggs lived here?

Walton Farm
Directly eastward is Walton Farm, (Plate 48) which was built by the Twiggs about 1800, around the time when they built the brickworks at Hazelstrine. The farmhouse had a very poor view of the surrounding area as it was hemmed in by farm buildings and brick walls. There was a spacious old barn, where the corn used to be ricked and thrashed out by hand. It had a paved way through the centre where the wagons could be drawn in, and the grain deposited from either side. True to the tradition of all the houses built by the Twiggs, it was described as " beautifully designed in every detail, with beauty and grace, achieved by hands which took a pride in their work"

Further east, on the land between the farm and School Lane, the Twiggs also built, at about the same time, a house known as Walton Rise. It was built on land owned by the Levetts for housing their agent.

The part of Walton we have still to review is the part known as "The Village". If we go back to "The Springs" and look at Map 4 it will be seen that there is an area which is bounded by the road from "The Springs" down to the "Pinfold", up to the corner on which the Church was built, down School Lane, and then joins up again at "The Springs". 18th-century Charity Records give the address of Richard Twigg as the "Pinfold". So was this plot of enclosed land just the "Pinfold", or was it, in these early days, the Village Green, as mentioned in a meeting of the Overseers of the Poor? At their meeting of 27th October 1801 they decided that stocks should be erected on the Village Green. If, because of the address, Richard Twigg did live there, he would have had a neighbour, as the Keelings had lived at Wysteria Cottage since the 17th century.

Plate 47 Mr & Mrs Woods outside PO circa 1899

Plate 48 Walton Farm

Before we go to the building of the church, just before we arrive at the church corner, a block of three terraced cottages was built, believed to be in the late 18th or early 19th century (Plate 49). It is thought they could have been built for farm labourers. A corner of the building juts out on to the road, which must have been a nuisance when this was the main road, particularly when the stage-coaches had to turn here. (Plate 49).

Plate 49 Three Terraced Cottages

Walton Church

Just across the road, at the start of School Lane, Walton Chapel-of-Ease was built in 1841/2, and dedicated to St.Thomas the Apostle, (Doubting Thomas). You will recall from the chapter on Baswich Church that it was proposed in 1808, that, instead of rebuilding Baswich Church, which was in a bad condition and in need of rebuilding, that consideration should be given to the alternative of building a church in a more central position. It had been suggested that the poor, who lived on the extremities of the parish, seldom, if ever, managed to get to church and were thus denied an opportunity of attending Divine Worship. Some thought had to be given as to whether it should be at Walton or Brocton, as the population growth at this time was concentrated in both of these villages, and it was anticipated that, whichever location was chosen, there would be disappointment at the other. Several plans were considered to meet the considerable expense which would be involved. The least objectionable proposal appeared to be to sell a sufficient part of Deepmore Common to meet this project, and also to sell more of the Common to build a "House of Industry". It appears that nothing eventuated from either proposal.

It was not until 1841 that a serious move was made to build the Chapel-of-Ease, when an Agreement was drawn up between the builder Thomas Trubshaw of Little Haywood, the Incumbent-in-Charge of the parish, the Rev. Leveson Lane, and the Rev. Richard Levett. It was dated January 25th.1841.

The cost, including labour, was to be £1841. The work was to be completed by 3rd October 1841. (This was for building a church without a tower and spire). It seems that they conjured some extra finance from somewhere, for a further Agreement was entered into, on June 5th, to enlarge the chancel and increase the thickness of the walls in that area, to enable them to add a tower, 12ft square, on top of which would be mounted a spire to a height of 27 ft. The cost of this additional work was £204 12s 0d. The inclusion of the extra work for the tower put back the completion date and the opening. The dedication service did not take place until 22nd December 1842.

The church was dedicated to St. Thomas the Apostle as a Chapel-of-Ease and consecrated by the Bishop of Hereford on behalf of the Bishop of Lichfield. (There is a story behind the latter's inability to officiate, but I think it prudent to omit it). The church was financed by Thomas Salt, who gave £200, and by the Rev. Richard Levett and his wife, Ann, who gave £150, and by public subscription.

The land on which the church was built was donated by the Earl of Lichfield. There was already a cottage adjacent to the site, built in 1730, which was extended to make the vicarage, which became the sole vicarage for the parish.

At the time the church was opened there was what was known as a "non-residential" Vicar, who did not himself perform the duties of the vicar in the parish, but appointed a Curate to act for him. At the date of opening, the Curate was Dr. Edgar Cross. When he left in 1844 he was succeeded by the Rev. H.B. Scougall, (Plate 50) whose period in charge came to a quick end when he was found to be having an affair with a Mrs. Wyatt from Acton Hill. (Harvey Wyatt was the Earl of Lichfield's Agent living at Acton Hill Farm). Mrs Wyatt went to live in North Wales, and the Curate went to live in Devon.

It was not the only event to reach the headlines whilst the Rev. Scougall was in charge. On Friday 9th May the church was struck by lightning. The "Illustrated London

Plate 50 Rev HB Scougall

News", issue dated 24th May 1845, carried the following report:-

"On the morning of Friday 9th May the village of Walton near Stafford was visited by a sharp thunderstorm, but singular to relate, only one clap of thunder was heard, and only one flash of lightning was seen. The fluid struck the spire of the church and destroyed part of it and melted the iron spouts on the south-west side, together with the glass in the windows, and shattered the window sills. A portion of the roof was likewise shattered." (Plate 51)

Plate 51 Walton Church struck by lightning in 1845

(It makes one wonder if the Patron Saint was not happy with what was going on).

The original stone structure of the spire was replaced by a wooden framework covered with lead in a diamond pattern.

Whilst there were some who "waxed lyrical" over the new church, others thought it had been built at the worst period of English architecture. One of the main criticisms was directed at the narrow lancet-type windows, which made the interior very gloomy. Understandable in the 1900s when lighting was by candles. The following is a sample of the lyrics mentioned, but others compiled by members of the Levett family are, in my opinion, too beautiful not to be published.

> *It standeth high upon a hill,*
> *How mighty it was placed,*
> *That we should lift our eyes to see,*
> *This house, this house of grace,*
> *Whoever built St.Thomas'*
> *Must surely had in mind,*
> *Lift up your eyes unto the hills,*
> *For there your help you'll find,*
> *Surrounded by green velvet sward,*
> *With lime trees standing guard,*
> *It stands alone, yet never so,*
> *For "tis the house of God".*

Salt School
Leaving the Church, within a short distance, connected by the path at the front of the vicarage, was the Salt School for children. It was opened by Miss Salt, of Weeping Cross, as a Dame School for young children.(Plate 52)

Plate52 Dame School

Almost opposite the Dame School a very high brick wall was built, both as a retaining wall and also as part of a large house called "Walton Lodge" It was built about 1730, and comprised of semi-detached lodges. In 1850 Judge Spooner occupied one, W. Morgan, a solicitor a second, and in 1853 John Hayes, Chief Constable made up the trio. (It appears a cosy little assembly of law men. There was a judge, a coroner, and a chief constable. One wonders if they ever conferred?)

Plate 53 Walton Lodge

Walton School

If we now continue down School Lane to the bend, just before it turns right, we would have found, in 1836, a plot of land, which the Earl of Lichfield had offered to give to the parish if a proposed school went ahead. A meeting was called for the 29th November 1836, by the Rev. Richard Levett at Milford Hall. Present were Rev. Levenson Lane, Rev. Richard Levett, Thomas Salt Esq., H. Wyatt Esq. (agent for the Earl of Lichfield.), and Rev. J.K. Stubbs. To summarise the agenda :-

"The principal inhabitants of the parish desired a school for the poorer children, based upon the teachings of the Church of England."

The Earl of Lichfield was giving the land and, to cover the cost, subscriptions would be necessary. Thomas Salt was appointed Treasurer; he would pay such subscriptions into the bank. A committee of subscribers would be formed, which would oversee the building plans, and a Mr. Tavenor would be asked to give an estimate of the cost of building the school and a school house.(Plate 54) An application would be made for union with the Central School Society, and for pecuniary aid from them. At a meeting on May 24th 1837, Mr. Tavenor's estimate of £250 for the building was accepted, and the building-work went ahead. It was estimated that the school would accommodate 74 children, both boys and girls.

When the school was opened, the headmaster was Mr. John Hines.

Plate 54 Walton School.

As we leave the school and cross over to the left hand side of the road to Milford, we soon come to the house of the Parish Clerk, Mr. George Thompson. The house has been extended on both sides since 1738 (Plate 55). When Mr. Thompson retired as Parish Clerk in 1840, he was presented with a silver plate and a bible. He was succeeded as Parish Clerk by his son who was a wheelwright.

Plate 55 Mr Thompson's House

Map 5 - Walton 1850 - 1920

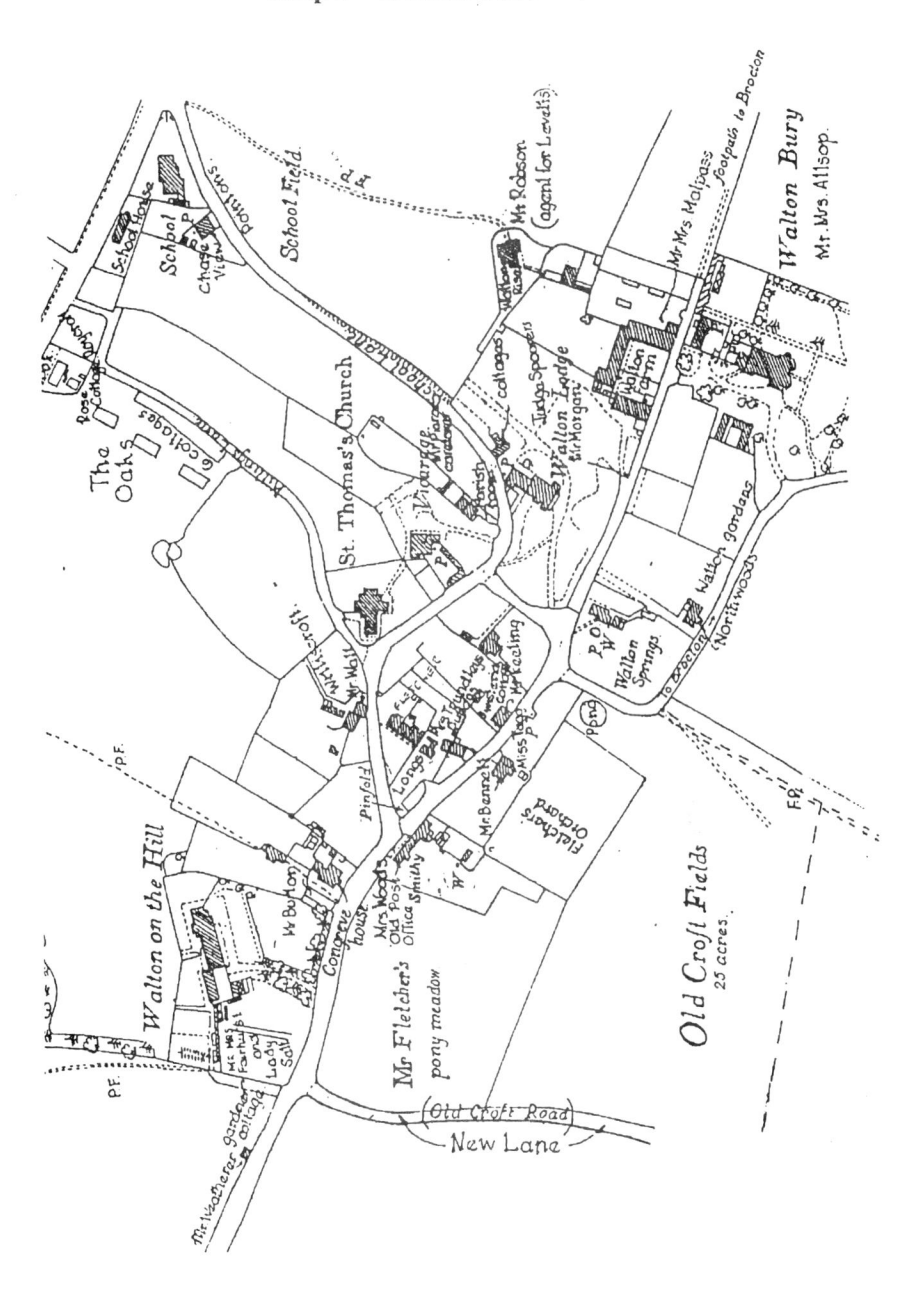

Chapter 7
STOCKTON & WALTON
(Part 2. 1850 to 1920)

In Stockton, between 1850 and 1920, there was little noticeable change.

As mentioned in the last Chapter the canal and railway came past the edge of the Common during that period. Besides the one house, already described, at the side of the canal, five cottages were built on the Common during the 19th century. It is thought that three were occupied by farm workers, and two by men employed on the railway track. Coming from the hamlet of Stockton towards the main Stafford to Lichfield road, six cottages (Plate 56) were built on the right hand side and, at the end of these, was a small grocery/sweet shop with a corrugated iron roof, run by a lady called "Mammy Green".

Plate 56 Cottages on Stockton Lane, looking towards the Lichfield Road.

Stockton Farm
As one almost reaches the main road, on the left-hand side was Stockton Farm (Plate 57), with Jno Kingstone as the farmer. Thomas Foster farmed there from 1892 to 1900, followed by Mr. & Mrs. Simon Bailey and their daughter Mary, who were there until 1910. From then until the time when we end this chapter, the Edwards's were there. I believe Mr. Edwards was still there when he died in 1938; the Harveys took over until

the farmhouse was knocked down, when the developers moved in, at this point the hamlet of Stockton lost its identity and disappeared.

On the opposite side of Stockton Lane, and facing the main road, was Stockton Croft.

Walton

As we leave Stockton and look back over the last century, it can be seen that the rate of change was very slow, quite in contrast to Walton where we move next. During the period 1850 to 1920, which we are looking at in this Section, the building of cottages went ahead at a steady pace. This was due mainly to what one could almost describe as the "Lords of the Manor" moving in. In the early part of this period the Bury was built, and the Allsops came. Later, Lady Salt arrived. The church vicarage had moved to Walton. The school had opened at the end of the 1830's, and there was Walton Farm. All these employed labourers, for whom cottages had to be built. So let us look at the changes in Walton since 1850.

Plate 57 Stockton Farm

Looking directly across the main road from Stockton Lane (see Map 1 - where we now see the start of Hillcroft Park), all that land was part of Stockton Farm. The field nearest the main road was known as "Front Field", and the two adjoining fields were approached by a track, which ran from the main road and ended at an old brick barn. There was a bullock yard at the back. On the right-hand side of the barnyard was a very deep well, (which, in the present day, would be to the right of Radstock Close). At the end of what is now Clevedon Avenue there was a small spinney, known as Evans' Wood. It was named after the owner of the fields adjoining the wood, who lived in a bungalow on the Lichfield-Road side of Baswich House.

If we now return to "Front Field", opposite Stockton Lane, and keep to the right-hand side of Walton Bank, (now called The Rise), the next field we come to was called "14 acre field". In the corner, where the Methodist Church now stands, was a pond, which sometimes had a pair of swans on it. At about where the drive entrance to Walton High School is, was a small three cornered field, with a stream running through it, called

"Tommy's Meadow" after the name of the pony. It was on "14 Acre field" that Walton High School was built.

If we cross over Walton Bank to the point where it joins the main road, in 1850 a new road was cut through from this point to just beyond the National School. As with all by-pass roads, the reason for it was to take the stage-coaches away from rumbling through the narrow winding road in the Walton village, particularly the acute bend near the church. But, too late; whilst the motor car had not made its debut in 1850, (the first one in these parts arrived in 1900), the railway line was opened almost as the road was being started. With the falling-off of stage-coach traffic it had come too late for the village.

Walton Garage

The motor car did eventually come, and the by-pass then became a blessing, not only for the motorist but for George Wood. About 1920 he took advantage of the sale of Army huts from the Brocton Camp, and erected the first Walton Garage.

Plate 58 Walton Garage

(Plate 58). In these early days of motoring, when Shell petrol sold in one-gallon cans at 1/3d. (6p), there were not enough cars about to make a proper living, although George's wife, Amy, helped, by making and selling sausages and pork pies from their bungalow. (In 1928 George sold out and went to work at Attwood's in Stafford).

A little further along the by-pass, on the other side of the road, was the beginning of the footpath, which went past the cottage of Giles the blacksmith. It passed through Stockton and across to Baswich. This formed the short route to Baswich Church for Walton residents.

Let us now rejoin Walton Bank and make our way into the village. At the start of this period, there would still be the beerhouse on the left at the top of the bank, and perhaps

John Harvey was still there, but, as seemed common to most of the villages, these beerhouses, in the early part of the 20th century, either closed, or took on a different trade. So it was more than likely that, by the time the Manor House changed hands, the beerhouse had gone.

Plate 59 "Walton on the Hill"

The next building at the top of Walton Bank was the Manor House, where, when we left it in the preceding Chapter, it was thought that Edward Harding lived. At the start of the 20th century it was occupied by Col. J. A. Fairhurst and his wife. Mrs Fairhurst was a daughter of the Ansell Brewery family. They left in 1905, and were followed by Lady Salt. After Sir Thomas Salt died in 1904, Lady Salt left Baswich House and took over what was the Manor House, renaming it "Walton-on-the-Hill", (Plate 59).

To direct people to her new home, Lady Salt had signposts erected on the by-pass, at the bottom of Walton Bank, and at the entrance to School Lane, which read "Walton-on-the Hill". The village of Walton, (which was spelt "Waltone" at the time of the Domesday Book in 1086), suddenly, apparently by the action of these signposts, became Walton-on-the Hill.

Lady Salt brought with her to Walton the staff who had served her at Baswich. She had four indoor servants and four outdoor, three of whom were gardeners, and the other was a man who looked after the plant which made the electricity for the house. For one of her gardeners, Arthur Weatherer, who also acted as chauffeur and handyman, she built a cottage just before the site of the beerhouse on Walton Bank. Mr. Weatherer had one daughter, Winnie, and her family remained in the village for many years. Lady Salt's wealth enabled her to buy six houses in the village, including the one where Mr. Fletcher, the village blacksmith, lived. Lady Salt left the village in 1920 and when she died she left many records to the William Salt Library. The next occupant of "Walton-on-the Hill" was Miss Brace.

We now move next door to Manor Farm. As far as can be ascertained, after the Congreves came the Kents, the Evans and the Burtons. The latter did not arrive until the 1930s, by which time the farming, on a small scale, was carried on by the daughters, as Mr. Burton's main trade was as a builder. One must assume, as happened elsewhere in the 20th century, that the farming aspect diminished, in many cases because the farming land was sold for building. The farm became more of a private residence than a farm. It is likely that whilst the Evans were there the residence became known as "Congreve House", and shortly afterwards all traces of its ever having been a farm disappeared. (Plate 60)

Plate 60 Congreve House

If we cross over to the opposite side of the road, named "The Village", it would be seen that there was only one house in New Lane (Old Croft Road), and this remained so until the 1920s. At the corner of New Lane and The Village, the old Blacksmith and cobbler's shop was pulled down around 1860 and a new blacksmith's shop was built next to the "Old Post Office".

WALTON POST OFFICE
Before we get to the smithy, we pass the thatched cottages where Smith, the blacksmith, and Genner, the cobbler lived. These were built in the 17th century. In 1900 the Woods family, who had run the Post Office at the "Springs", moved in, and in doing so established it as Walton Post Office, (See Plate 45 on page 70). It belonged to Lord

Lichfield's estate and his agent allowed them to live there, rent-free, for one year because of the poor condition of the place. After they had done it up, they were allowed to continue to live there for a rent of 2/6d (12p) per week. The Woods had four children, Walter, Bill, George and Marguerite (Rita). (Plate 62 shows Rita with her mother). The father, Samuel Woods, ran a painting and decorating business from the rear of the Post Office. Plate 61 shows Samuel Woods with Bill, Rita, and George Woods. Rita married a Mr. Ashcroft in 1924, and went back to live in the "Springs", where she had been born in 1895. Samuel Woods, died in 1932, and his wife Katherine continued to run the Post Office. She died in 1941.

Plate 61 Woods at Back of Post Office

The Village Blacksmith

Thomas Fletcher was the new blacksmith, and he had his stepson, Joe, to help him. He came to Walton from Acton where he spent eight years learning his trade. His father was coachman to the first Lord Hatherton, and Lady Hatherton paid the premium when the young Thomas was apprenticed. In addition to being blacksmith he was also the village "pinner", and kept stray animals in the Pinfold opposite his shop, until they were claimed. He lived in the end house of a terrace of three, which had been built in the triangle in the centre of the village. (Plate 63) His neighbours were Mr. Beech, who worked for Lady Salt, and Mrs. Dutton. At the end of this row was the cottage in which Mrs. Trundley lived, she lost her only son in the First World War.

Mr. Beech's house was a gift from the Salt family. It was beautifully furnished with furniture and china from a past age. When Lady Salt left he was allowed to have

Plate 62 Mrs K Woods & daughter Rita

anything he wished from the house. He told many stories of the old days, the food and its preparation, and the large dinner parties which they had in the big house. They also had some lovely parties in the servant's hall. Mr. Beech lived in the village from the time when Lady Salt moved in until his death in 1951.

Back to Thomas Fletcher the blacksmith. He was the only blacksmith in the parish, so there was a variety of horses, which were brought to him to be shod; cart-horses, ponies, hunters etc., but his skills went as far as making iron railings, children's hoops and repairing cart-wheels. Plate 64 is of Mr Fletcher and an apprentice Ben Tooth outside the Smithy. When not busy in his forge, he kept chickens in the pony-meadow which stretched from the back of the blacksmith's shop to New Lane. He was a bell-ringer at Baswich church for more than 60 years. He retired when he was 70, and enjoyed a long retirement, which he spent in his garden and orchard. He often admitted he had been lucky in his general health. Once when he was young he had suffered from sciatica. It was cured by the village doctor who put one of his irons in the smithy fire and then gave him four dabs with it on his back. He never had sciatica again. At the age of 90 he was pruning the trees in his orchard on the day when he died in 1942.

Leaving the blacksmith's shop, and just a little further on the same side are two cottages in front of Mr. Fletcher's orchard (Plate 65). In the first lived Mr. Bennett, who was gardener to Mr. Morgan at Walton Lodge. Next door lived Miss Tagg, another of the well-known characters of the village. She was a teacher at the National School, a Sunday School teacher and a member of the Walton Church Choir. One of the choirboys, who sat behind her, stuck a sticky sweet to the rim of her hat. As he also went to the National

Plate 63 Thomas Fletcher's House

Plate 64 Mr Fletcher outside the Smithy

School, he paid for his prank on the Monday morning.

Miss Tagg had a sister, Lydia, who was fourteen years older. It seems that, although she lived to 90, only a few people in the village knew of her, even though she had attended the Betty Dean School at Milford. (The Betty Dean School features later).

Wysteria Cottage

Opposite to Miss Tagg's cottage was "Wysteria Cottage". You will remember from the previous Chapter that Hales Keeling was living there in 1694. After him came Sampas Keeling, who became the village postmaster. He died in 1891 and a tribute in the Church Magazine read :-

"A familiar figure has passed away in the person of Sampas Keeling of the Post Office, Walton. The south transept of Walton Church seems desolate and deserted without him. He was a man with the strongest sense of duty, and to the last, in spite of increasing infirmities, would not let another do his Post Office work. 'The ruling passion' it is said, is 'strong in death'. It was so with him. During the last struggle, he was constantly, in imagination, making up the post bag and exclaiming 'Is the bag ready'. He led a truly, godly, righteous and sober life and we trust he has now entered into peace. "

His son, John, continued to live at "Wysteria Cottage", behind which he cultivated a market-garden, and took produce to Stafford for sale on market-days. He played a prominent part in church life, being bellringer and caretaker for many years. He died on 9th April 1925 aged 71, and was buried in Baswich churchyard. Plate 46 taken in 1910, shows John at the door. "The Springs" can be seen in the background.

Plate 65 Miss Tagg's & Mr Bennett's Cottages

If, after leaving "Wysteria Cottage", we take the turn on the right, we go past "Spring Cottage", which belonged to the Allsopps of Walton Bury. It became the Post Office in 1891 when Samuel and Katherine Woods moved in, and they stayed there until 1900 before moving to No.14, The Village.

If you continued a short distance after passing Spring Cottage, (you can see this on Map 5), you would see a pond on the right. Then you would come to a bend in the road which continued to Brocton. Just on the bend was the "Kissing Gate" and beyond, on the right, was a large oak tree, which had been planted in 1837 to commemorate the Coronation of Queen Victoria. Here was the start of a footpath, which forked to the right to the Old Croft cricket field and pavilion. To go straight on led to the Cannock road, a path well-worn by the men of the village on their way to the "Seven Stars" public house, and a similar target for the cricketers at the end of a match.

Walton Cricket Club

Plate 66 Cricket Team 1886

In the summer months, the cricket field was a popular venue for the men of the village, and the Walton Cricket Club could field both well-known names and excellent players. The first club started about 1880 and was captained by Mr. R.H. Hand. (Plate 66) It was revived in 1904 by Col. J. A. Fairhurst and Mr. W.W. Morgan with Sir Thomas Salt as President, and Mr. Henry Twigg and Mr. W. Morgan as Vice-Presidents. In 1906 Capt. the Hon. H.T. Allsopp became Vice President. Walton Cricket Weeks became a great attraction, which regrettably came to an abrupt end, on August 4th. 1914, when many of the members joined the armed forces. Captain Allsopp was a Cambridge blue, and the

Vicar, the Rev. F.G. Inge, was an Oxford blue. Of the well-known names in the parish, who played for Club and County were the three Twiggs - C.H. Twigg, F.W. Twigg and W.H. Twigg; also, three of the Morgan family, R.G.O. Morgan, G.W.R. Morgan and W.W. Morgan, who revived the club after the First World War when it moved to Milford. (The Walton Heights housing estate had been built upon the Old Croft Field).

The same field,, which was the cricket pitch in the summer was the football pitch in the winter. In 1907, the Curate, Rev. Capell, enjoyed playing in both sports, but he made known his feelings about soccer and its supporters when he wrote in the Church Magazine:-

"The supporters are most enthusiastic in support of their club, and I think a little cheering helps, but at times it goes beyond that, and is the cause of some of the rough play which takes place. For example, the other day I had the misfortune to play in goal when a penalty was given against us. When the opposing player failed to score there was laughter and rude remarks. Whilst I felt thankful for the miss, I do hope that in future the spectators will not incite dirty play and show appreciation for good play. It may only be thoughtlessness, but bad manners spring from that"

Things don't change much!

Plate 67 Mr Northwood's House Brocton Lane

We won't take the footpath to the "Seven Stars". Instead we will go back through the "Kissing Gate" and turn right into Brocton Lane. The field on the right, known as "Gorsty Field" was the site of the celebrations for the Coronation of Queen Victoria. They had a maypole for the children, and other events. (This is the site of the present Primary School).

The first house, which we see on the left, was built by Captain Allsopp of Walton Bury, in 1908, for the parents of Mrs. Woods, (of the post office), who were named Crookes. Mr. Crookes was gardener for the Bury. They stayed for less than two years, and then Richard and Jane Northwood, with their four children, moved in on the 1st October 1909, (Plate67). Mr. Northwood, who came as a trained Head Gardener, was paid the princely sum of only 30/- (£1.50)per week.

Walton Bury

Plate 68 Walton Bury

Within a few yards, at the slight bend in the road, the drive to Walton Bury came into view. The house was built in 1880, on land leased from the Earl of Lichfield, by the "Master Builders" of the parish, the Twiggs, and, true to their tradition, it was a solidly-built house with huge windows throughout, and those at the front of the house gave a view across to the hills of Wales.(Plate 68).

The first occupants were Captain, the Hon. H.T. Allsopp and his wife, The Hon. Mrs. E.M. Allsopp (Plate 69) Captain Allsopp was an officer in the Hussars, and was the 5th son of the 1st Baron Hindlip of Hindlip Hall, Worcester. The Hon. Mrs. Allsopp was a Miss Okeover of Okeover Hall, Ashbourne, one of a family of seven. They had a daughter, Cynthia, who was born in 1895. She remained a spinster, and, like the whole of the family, played a prominent part in the activities of the parish and the local church.

Plate 69 Hon Mrs EM Allsop

The south transept of the church was regarded as the exclusive domain of the Allsopp family and their staff. The stained glass window, which was a gift from them, bore evidence of their involvement. They entered by an exclusive side-door, which had a dog gate. The choir boys regarded The Hon. Mrs. Allsopp as "eagle-eyed", for they said she was always watching them and reporting them to the vicar if they misbehaved. The Hon. H.T. Allsopp was a good cricketer, and also enjoyed rowing his boat on the river Sow. In both World Wars the Bury was used as a First Aid Centre. The Hon. Mrs. Allsopp died in 1935 and her daughter, Cynthia, in 1974.

Walton Farm

If we take the back way out of the Bury, into the footpath which leads both to Brocton and to Jacob's Ladder, directly in front of us is Walton Farm, which was covered in the previous Chapter. Since 1850 there are many changes. The big barn has been converted into flats. The first farmer was a Mr. Malpass. He was succeeded by his son Harry, who married the daughter of Mr. Edwards of Stockton Farm in 1913. Harry was the tenant farmer there from 1915 to 1938. When he took over the farming was mostly arable, but changed to dairy farming in time to meet the demands for milk from the Army Camp, which had been built at Brocton. Milk was delivered locally by pony-drawn milk-float. When the war ended in 1918 supplies were diverted, by rail, to larger dairies.

At the rear of Walton Farm, reached by the footpath from School Lane, was another house built by one of the Twiggs for Captain Levett which was called "Walton Rise" In the early 20th century this was occupied by Mr. Robson who was agent for Captain Levett.

Plate 70 Farnworth Brothers Cottages

We now retrace our steps back to the Old Post Office corner and turn to the right. Immediately opposite we see a pair of semi-detached cottages. (Plate 70). During the time that Lady Salt was at "Walton-on-the Hill", two of her gardeners, the Farnsworth brothers, lived there, but when she left in 1920 they were followed by Mr. & Mrs Clements. Within a few yards we come to what was, originally, a terrace of three

Plate 71 Originally farm-workers cottages

farm-workers cottages of oakbeam construction. At a later date the walls were plastered over and ultimately they became one house (Plate 71) An outstanding feature is that the south corner juts out into the road and must have been quite an obstacle when the stage coaches ran past there where the road was so narrow. There is no record of who the early occupants were, but in the early 20th century they were Mr. Hemmings, (followed by Miss Ball) Mr. Dawson and Mr. Wall. (followed by Mrs. Mahon) All of these old cottages had to rely on oil-lamps for lighting until 1915, and their water came from the village pump. At the east side there was another cottage occupied by Mr. Willistcroft. In his spare time he was a scoutmaster and arranged many trips to the seaside for local boys.

Immediately left, a lane, which was called Kitlings Lane, ran down to the main road. In the 19th and early 20th centuries there were no houses on the right; there was a field which stretched from the church walls to School Lane and down to the main road. On the left were six cottages known as "The Oaks", and in one of these lived the Curate to the Vicar, the Rev. Inge. The Curate was the Rev. D'Ombrain and he married one of the Misses Twigg from Weeping Cross. (Over the years at least four Curates and one Vicar have married girls from the parish. One escaped).

At the bottom of the lane there were two cottages fronting the main road, and to the right was the village "tuck" shop, run by Mrs G Pierce (Plate 72). A little further to the right was the headmaster's cottage. Across the road was Green Gore Lane. The Village Hall was not in existence at this time, for it was later, in 1921, when such a

Plate 72 Village 'Tuckshop'

building was suggested, and Capt. Levett offered to give the land required if the suggestion went ahead.

Plate 73 Village Hall Committee
Back Row: Mr S Lewis, Miss Tagg, Mr HF Sadlier, Mrs E Cook, Mr WJ Shepherd,
Mr HJ Clay, Mrs B Wilson, Miss Birks, Alderman HJ Bostock
Front Row: Mr FE Thewlis, Mr W Bream, Lady Lichfield, Mrs DR Haszard, Rev G Hitchings.

Walton Church

We now have to go back to the other end of Kitlings Lane, to the church. In the previous Chapter we covered the building of the church and the opening in 1842. After the Rev Scougall left in 1857, the church passed through a quieter period under the Rev Charles Steward (Plate 74). When he left in 1865, the Rev. Charles Edward Drew arrived (Plate 75). It was the Rev. Drew who initiated the Parish magazine, "The Three Decker".

The previous Chapter detailed the building of the church, its opening in 1842, and the building of a new spire to replace the one struck by lightning in 1845. The next major happening to the building was not until 1903, when it was found that the spire was unsafe because it was too heavy. The lead covering was removed and replaced with a lighter metal in an herringbone design. The weathercock, besides being too heavy, did not function correctly because of the weight and was replaced with a lighter version (Plate 76). Whilst the work was being carried out, regular prayers were said for the safety of the steeplejacks.

Plate 74 Rev Charles Steward   Plate 75 - Rev Charles Drew

The discarded weathercock became a garden ornament in the garden of the vicarage, and it stood there in peace until we had a vicar with three sons and one air-rifle. The weathercock then became the target for their practice, and when they left it looked a sorry sight. In time all of the indentations were filled, and it found an honourable resting place on the roof of the boiler-house. Plate 77 shows the church with its new spire, in the foreground the Vicarage, which was converted from an existing cottage and enlarged to make a vicarage at the time of the building of the Church. It will be noticed that a field, under cultivation, went right up to the churchyard wall.

THE THREE DECKER
In the first edition, dated September 1882, the Rev. Drew said that he wanted a "*direct means of communication*", and a record of events within the parish. The first editions comprised a single folded sheet, with news on two or three of the pages. The next development was the folded sheet, as above, with a nationally-produced insert called "Banner of Faith", a fascinating production containing a serial, short stories and articles, which all seemed to have strongly pointed morals and a bigoted outlook on anything which did not conform to the teaching of the Established Church. Also included were some full pages of "Health Hints", ranging from making Poultices and Fomentations to putting a sheet of brown paper on the back and then using a warm iron to iron over it, to get rid of backache. It is hard to imagine the degree of wonderment raised in the minds of people who read the Science Jottings, e.g. "*Electricity-the power which is rapidly making this old world young again. It is so awesome because it cannot be seen and runs*

down copper wires. It will even activate a thing called an electric motor which will replace the power of steam."

In 1902 there is a report of the invention of the Phonograph, on which, it says, people will be able to record voices which can be heard later. But how clever these Victorians were when an article informs us that lamp posts were being erected in busy centres. Heat from the gas lamps would be used to heat water in a tank. Small packets of tea would be provided and, by inserting a half-penny, one would be able to enjoy a cup of tea.

The introduction and editing of these magazines remained in the hands of the vicar for generations. One supposes that this was a safeguard, but later vicars did not want to know. They were quite happy to write what was called "Vicarage Viewpoint", and to trust that there were enough members willing to form a committee and do the work he did not want to do. (Today it is called "passing the buck").

Plate 76 Replacing the Spire in 1903

The man who introduced the magazine, the Rev. Charles Drew left in 1884 with the good wishes of the parish, and they presented him with a silver tobacco-jar. The school children presented him with a bound copy of Keble's "Lyra Innocentium".

On the 3rd February 1884, following the death of the non-resident Vicar, The Rev. T. Levenson Lane, the Bishop of Lichfield instituted the Rev. Francis George Inge as Vicar. He was a member of a well known family, the Inges of Thorpe. Like all of the Vicars and Curates, who had preceded him, he had a very impressive beard, and, in build and stature, was a "double" for the legendary W. G. Grace. (Strange to relate, he was also the last vicar in the parish to wear a beard). Such a description was indeed very suited to the man for he was an Oxford Blue. He played a brilliant game of cricket, and did all in his power to encourage village cricket. He was, during his active years, a great asset to Walton Cricket Club.

Plate 77 St Thomas' Church with new Spire

The Rev. Inge (Plate 78) arrived in the parish as a single and attractive man, and one would have thought that, with the number of unmarried daughters of well-known families in the district, he would have had little difficulty in finding a wife. His first attempt was not successful. One Sunday he walked to Milford, and proposed to the lady of his choice. She refused him. (Whilst the Levett family would neither confirm nor deny that it was one of the Levett girls, there was always a suspicion that it was.) He was apparently not the man to have only one string to his bow, so he returned "hot-foot" to Walton, perhaps fortified himself with drink, and said a little prayer, and then walked across the lane to Walton Lodge and knocked at the door of Judge Spooner. "Hello Vicar", said the Judge, "What can I do for you?" "I would like to speak to your daughter, Catherine, please" He proposed, she accepted. She was used to Vicars, for her brother was the "Gloomy Dean" of St. Paul's, famed for his "Spoonerisms"; one of the well-known sayings was "Cats never hurt themselves when falling for they always pop on their draws". Gloomy he might have been, but he agreed to give his sister away at the wedding which took place on the 11th November 1884 at St. Giles' Church, Oxford. The groom's brother, the Provost of Worcester College Oxford officated, assisted by the bride's uncle, the Very Revd. E. Spooner, Rector of Hadleigh.

When they returned from their honeymoon in the pony and trap, which was his regular mode of travel, local friends took the horse from the shafts and drew the trap through the gates of the vicarage, where the happy couple were pelted with rice. It turned out to be a happy marriage, but a childless one. Mrs Inge devoted herself to the life of the parish and, with her husband, would prepare breakfast for anyone who came to early morning service.

After 28 years as Vicar of Berkswich, and with increasing deafness, he retired, at the age of 71, to Oxford. His period at Berkswich was regarded as having the stabilising effect which the parish, at that time, so badly needed.

The Rev. Inge was succeeded by the Rev. Story Busher of Kings Bromley, who only stayed a little over 2 years, but in that time he took the opportunity of finding himself a local bride. He married Miss Alice Mabel Twigg of Weeping Cross. (This was the second of the Twigg girls to marry into the church. The first married a Curate).

Plate 78 Rev & Mrs F G Inge

The Rev. Busher was succeeded, in 1914, by the Rev. Gerald Hitchings. He came as a single man and left in 1933 still a bachelor.

During this period, 1850 to 1920, there were changes in the church. In 1882 the Levetts gave windows as a memorial to Miss Levett and, in 1889, as a memorial to Colonel Levett. Between 1886 and 1888 they had the walls coloured, and decorated with a biblical text over the chancel arch which read :- *"We praise Thee, we bless Thee, we give thanks to Thee for thy great glory, O Lord God Heavenly King",* and also paid for 100 new hassocks.

It was a sad time for the Levetts when, in 1917, Lieut. Richard Byrd Levett, aged 19, was killed in action on March 10th. He was the only son of Capt. and Mrs. Levett. The same sorrow was felt by many other families in the parish, and the names of those who gave their lives in the Great War 1914-18, are engraved in the memorial chapel in the church, and on the Memorial Cross at Weeping Cross, mentioned in an earlier Chapter.

Ancient Parish of Berkswich.

As a lasting memorial to their son, Capt. and Mrs. Levett commissioned the beautiful marble memorial of the sleeping figure of Richard Byrd Levett, in soldier's uniform, which was placed at the entrance to the North Chapel. The Levetts asked that the chapel should be known as the Memorial Chapel, dedicated to St. George. At the entrance, above the memorial tomb, there was erected a canopy in limed oak.

The transformation of the North Chapel actually restored the entrance to the chancel to how it had been when the church was built. In 1842 the pulpit was on the south side, and the vicar entered the pulpit, through a hole in the wall from the vestry. (The outline of this entrance can be seen in the plaster today). It was changed sometime in the 1880s, when the Rev. Inge and his wife, with members of their families, donated the screen and pulpit of stone and alabaster. At the same time the pulpit was moved to the north side.

As with most churches at this time, they were cold and dark, and whilst a huge coke-burning stove had been installed in Walton Church, it was some years before electric lights appeared.

At the end of this review of the church came a milestone in democracy within the Church. On December 1919 the Enabling Act was passed, by which the running of the church passed into the hands of a newly-elected Parochial Church Council (PCC).

Salt School
We now leave the church and pass along School Lane. At the beginning of the period under review, 1850, we would find, on our left, the Salt School for Infants, supported entirely by Miss Salt, and mistressed by Mrs. Keeling. Whilst it had places for 40 children, the average attendance in 1840 was 20. Children were taught here up to the age of eight, and then they were passed to the Dame School at Milford, where they were accepted by the Levetts, who paid for their schooling.

The Salt school closed down in 1894 because of the Education Act, and the building became a "Parish Room". It continued to be used for some lessons by the National School and also by the Church. The caretaker, Mr. Dawson lived in the end room.

At the bottom of the lane was a cottage, which was the home of a retired couple, Mr. & Mrs. Pointon. Just before the cottage was a field, in which Mr. Pierce kept pigs. Later Mr. Pierce built a house on the field and sold off the remainder of the land for building.

Walton Church of England School
Next we come to the National School, which had changed a good deal since we left it in 1850.

The Education Act of 1870 had caused some problems, since in order to qualify for a grant from the Government, the school had to be enlarged to meet Government standards. Also the grant was based on average attendances. In the past the School had been troubled with parents keeping their children at home for all kind of reasons. The cost of extending the school was raised by public subscription, and was opened in October 1894 with a service of dedication by the Bishop of Lichfield.

The School was not free of its problems, mainly from the school being closed because of measles in 1885, redecoration in 1887, and the resignation of teachers. Most problems seemed to come to an end with the appointment of Mr. Longson as Headmaster in 1895, with his wife as Headteacher. There are records of pupils starting to receive prizes for excellence. Mr. Longson formed a strong bond with the church and arranged for the pupils to attend services, and he helped, when required as organist. Mrs. Longson was very kind to the children. When the weather was wet she would dry the clothes of the children in front of the school stove and, when cold, she would make hot soup for them. The ladies of the village, (Miss Salt, Miss Tagg and the Levett girls), were regularly inspecting the school, and teaching sewing and singing.

Plate 79 Mr & Mrs Longson

During the Great War, 1914-1918, school-dinners were provided for the children by Mrs. Longson and the girls of the cookery class at a cost of 10d per week.

Mr. and Mrs. Longson gave 35 years teaching and caring for the children of Walton and district. (Plate 79). They were much loved by everyone. When they retired in August 1926 they were presented with a fine French carriage-clock.

This ends the first part of our tour. The second part picks up the story at Milford, takes in Shugborough, Brocton, Acton, Bednall and Teddesley Hay, all part of the "Ancient Parish of Berkswich".

Appendix 1
Assessment of Scrap Value of Baswich Church in 1803

James Varley's Valuation of the Old Materials of the Old Church at Berkswich.

	£. s. d
Four Walls, Roof, and Slating	45. 16. 0
170 Yards of Tile Covering	8. 10. 0
Lead Gutters in Church Roof	9. 0. 0
174 Yards of Brick Work at 340 Bricks per Yard	60. 19. 0
200 Feet of Stone Plinth at 6. per Foot	5. 0. 0
200 Feet of Cornice at 1.6 per Foot	15. 0. 0
15 Squares at 2. 10. 0 per Square	37. 10. 0
Ceiling Joists 10 Squares at 5/ per Square	2. 10. 0
Iron Rods or Saddle Bars for Windows 300 at 3. per lb	3. 15. 0
200 Feet of Glass and Lead at 6. per Foot	5. 0. 0
2 Doors, Frames, and Hinges	2. 0. 0
1078 Feet of Pews at 10. per Foot	44. 18. 4
300 Feet of Seats in Pews at 6. per Foot	7. 10. 0
Pulpit 216 Feet at 1.6 per Foot	16. 4. 0
Stone in Doors, Windows, and Stair cases	13. 14. 0
	£277. 6. 4

Appendix 2
Inventory of all the things of the Chapel and Sacristy
1684-1688 - Inventory of Contents of St Thomas' Priory

<u>Inventory of all the things of the Chapel and Sacristy</u>

Pictures

The altar piece; Our Saviour and Our Lady; Our lady with Our Saviour in her arms; St. Monica; Our Saviour taken down from the Cross; St. Thomas of Canterbury; St. Lawrence; St. Dominic and St. Thomas of Aquin; St. Peter and St. Mary Magdalen; St. Francis and St. Veronica; one little picture of Mrs Fowler and six paper pictures in frames.

Wooden Work

An altar table; two cretensall tables; one great chair; six great forms; two little forms; one tabernacle; two great stands to set before the altar, with salvers for candles; two less stands for the Paschal and the three Marys; two steps with several drawers according to the colours ofd the feastsfor the altar candlesticks to stand on; one press to keep the chalice in; one great press to keep the vestments in; several triangular sticks to hold them in; one great press to vest on; one box to keep the flowers in; one box for the veils; one box for the frames which are set under the tabernacle; two little tables; one great box to keep the altar linen in; one triangular frame for Tenebrae; one reliquary which hangs on the vesting table.

Candlesticks

Six silver candlesticks with six salvers; one silver cretensall candlestick; one silver bell; one silver; pax; one silver plate for the cruets; one silver cup for the communicants; six long pewter candlesticks for the altar; one small one for elevation; four bigger for the cretensall tables; three for the hearse; two more for use; two hanging ones over the rail; one pair of snuffers with a plate; two candlesticks of white ware; several pots of white ware for flowers.

Vestments

One green vestment with maniple and stole; three white vestments with maniples and stoles; three red vestments with maniples and stoles; one purple vestment with maniple and stole; two black vestments with maniples and stoles; one calico vestment with maniple and stole; one cope, one mitre, one corner cap; three gowns.

Antependiums

Two white ones; three red ones; one green one; two black ones; one purple one; one calico one; with stools in frames for each cretensall conformable to the vestments.

Inventory of all the things of the Chapel and Sacristy

Veils

One green one; three red ones; two white ones; two black ones; one purple and one for the calico suit.

Carpets, cushions for the altar, hangings in the Chapel

One old carpet which is daily used; one new carpet for great feats; one black carpet of cloth; one pair of red curtains for the altar, with a rod; one pair of black silk curtains; four red altar cushions, two of them twisted; two green ones twisted; two black ones; two white ones; two purple ones; two calico ones; two black covers for the hearse; two cloths with death heads for the cross on the hearse; four black covers for the forms; three great hangings without the rail; black hangings with strips of gilt leather within the rail.

Borders and linen for the altar

One border called Heads and Heels; one called Aunt Mary's border; one cambric altar cloth laced; one scalloped altar cloth; one plain altar cloth; the same of each altar cloth for the cretensall tables; two covers to the altar, one laced; two long communion cloths, two lesser ones; one surplice; two girdles; three albs; four amices and two diaper napkins; two flaxen napkins and six side towels to wipe the fingers; two linen bags for the chalice; one broad sheet under the altar cloth, also one calico, and a diaper one under the altar cloth; one sheet on the vesting table; one sheet on the chalice table, and a sheet in the box; one laced under-altar cloth.

Heirlooms in the Chapel

One silver cross; one little gold cross; one gilted chalice and platen; one altar stone.

What belongs to Mrs. Gertrude Fowler

One silver cup for communion; one needleworked border used on the black antependium; one white satin border; one white bossed satin vestment with maniple and stole; one red vestment with a lacy gold lace; and a red antependium with a gold glorie; one black vestment with a silver lace on it, and an antependium with a silver glorie on it; two sets of flowers being the best used on great feasts, and the ordinary ones on weekdays with earthen pots; two reliquaries with gilted frames for the tabernacle.

Inventory of all the things of the Chapel and Sacristy
(Page 3)

What belongs to Mr. Dan Fitters in the Chapel at St. Thomas

[This section was inserted in Francis Fitter's hand after the rest of the inventory had been made.]

One big silver gilt chalice with a silver gilt paten to it.

This was bought with Mr. Daniel Fitters' money though it came not to the chapel till after his death where it was intended by him to be used during Mr. William Fowler's life only, after which to be delivered up for the use of the clergy only in this district.

For the Chapel

One gilted cross on the altar; one silver lamp; one silver thurible; two silver towers for perfumes; one silver pax; two wooded reliquaries on the cretensall tables with the relics in them; one statue of Our Lady; one white vestment which has an embroidery of figures on the back, having a broad lace about it; a white antependium with stools; one worse red vestment with maniple and stole; four tin perfuming pans; all the gilted flower pots; one set of spangle flowers; one great carpet of St. George; two lesser carpets used every Sunday; three borders, one of crimson, one of white satin with high bosses; three of red silk, with a lace about it; two pictures in gilted frames, one of the Garden, the second of the Pillory; two pictures of St. Peter and St. Paul; one of St. Sebastian; one of St. Barbara; all the canopy sets.

* * * * * * *

Appendix 3
Extract from Constable's Accounts 1701

ACCOUNTS of CONSTABLE 1701-1756

EDWARD HALTON

"The Accounts of the Constable of Walton beginning the 3 day of October in 1700 and ending the 22 of October in 1701"

		s.	d.
1701	Paid for this book	2.	6
	My charges to the Court and my oath	1.	4
	The Head Borah charges and my oath	1.	4
	Paid to the Malisha and small payments	14.	0
	My charges and aquittance	1.	4
	For going to Canock to give in a list of the maltsters and badgers to take	1.	0
	Paid to the head constable for passing away of vagrants at Penkridge	5.	2
	For my charges and acquittance	1.	4
	For going to a Monthly Meeting and putting in my presentment against the sessions	1.	4
	Paid to the head constable for the passing away of vagrants and for the Bread for the priffonor (prisoner) and my acquittance	5.	5
			4
	For my charges and putting in my	1.	8
	For going to a Monthly Meeting	1.	0
	Paid for smal payments & acquittances	2.	4
	For a Book of Articolls	1.	0
	For going to a Monthly Meeting	1.	0
	Paid to the head constable for passing of vagrants & removing the inhabitants from Chyslin Hay & for Bread for prisoner & for my acquittance	9.	1
			4
	For going to a Monthly Meeting & for putting in my at sessions	1.	8
	Paid Malisha money & acquittance for going	12.	4
	to a Monthly Meeting & putting in a against the assizes	1.	8
	Paid to the head constable for passing away of vagrants & Brigg moneys	9.	2
	For closing the Shire Hall & my acquittance		
	Paid a Monthly Meeting last for small payments due at Michaelmas	2.	0
	My charges & acquittances	1.	4
	For one load of colle for William Bruce	5.	6
	Paid for a warrant	5.	0
	Paid for the Town Muskit Mending	1.	6
	and scouring the sword & newgrabout	2.	6
	For the laying a lown & writting	1.	6
	For going before a Justice with Sarah Buffot & the Head borrow (borough) with & for going for an order to remove her. Fetching her daughter from Stafford & maintaining her all night & for carrying her away to Sutton & for maintenance upon the way	15.	6
	I gave her children at parting	1.	0

Appendix 4
Churchwardens' and Overseers' Account Book

NOTES of CHURCHWARDENS' and OVERSEERS' ACCOUNT
BOOK - 1699-1740

The hand writing varies a good deal owing to changes in the holders of the office.
In general the accounts open with a statement of initial expenses, and conclude with a charge ``for writing my accounts and giving them up''.
Regular payments include -
Expenses on the first and second Visitation
by the Dean; also
For Bread and Wine for Communion, certain Charities
and various expenses including Payments for
vermin destroyed and various loads of coal;
Frequent small charges for oyle for the Bells.

Throughout the period the Bells were rung on the 5th November, the Bell Ringers being paid 1/6d.
There are frequent entries for drawing Deepmor Ditch.
The Opening Entry is -
"Accompts of Edward Hall, Churchwarden and Overseerer of the Poore for the Constabellwirk of Woolton begining Aprill the eleaventh Anno Dommino 1699".

Among the interesting entries are -

```
1703   Pd for a prayer book & a procklimacion (Queen Anne)  1.  6
       Pd for a fox head                                    1.  0
       Pd for a book the Day of the Queen )
       Coming to the Crowne              )                      6
       Pd for 23 hedghogs                                   3. 10
       Pd for 34        and 9 sparrows                      2. 10¼

1704   Pd for washing of Ann Howell                         4.  0
       Pd for charg of Buryall of Ann Howell & Looking to her 7. 5

1726   For my jurney to Pilington for a warrand for Tho Tomson
         labarer and his wife for abusive words             1.  0
       Pd to Rich Twigg for a horse to fetch the midwife        6
         for my going                                           6
       Pd for a horse for Tho Wordley           £1. 15.  0

1744   For bleeding Ann Wardley                                 6
       Pd to a big beled woman                              1.  0
       Pd for too hancerchifes for Ann Wardley              1.  4

1779   Pd to John Green in illness                          5.  0
       Pd for a sroude                                      3.  6
       Pd for Green's coffin                                8.  0
```

Cont'd

Churchwardens' and Overseers' Account Book
(Page 2)

1768	Pd for 2 forms of prayer for the Queen *(Wife of George III)*	1.	6
1786	Pd for a form of thanksgiving for George III	1.	0

1795   Expences in Eateing & Drinking in Various places
       with John Salt   6.   0
       Marriage Licence for John Salt and Mary Sutton   £1. 15. 0
       Wager lost with John Salt   2. 2. 0

1801
Oct 27 At a meeting held this day at the home of Sam Copestick at Weeping Cross, it was resolved that a house should be opened for the reception of the poor of the parish of Baswich, and that the buildings offered by Mr Micheal Harding, at the annual rent of six pounds six shillings for the above purpose be engaged against Lady Day next.
(This is the first mention of a Workhouse in Walton)

                                                                                             £   s   d
      Paid Mr Harding for Thatching the Workhouse   10. 0. 0
           Edw. Vickers for 3 Bed Matts for –do–   9. 0
           W. Hall for work at the Workhouse   15. 4
           Mr Boulton for 3 Bed Ticks etc etc   2. 5. 0

1811
      That George Thompson and John Hughes be appointed Overseers of the Poor of the said parish.

1812
      Rent on the Workhouse   8. 0. 0

1813
      The Bond for Mary Dutton's Bastard child was burnt by the gentlemen assembled. The Bond entered into by Joseph Pickin and his two brothers, one of whom (the reputed father of the child is dead) he having paid all the arrears at this time.

1816
Oct 27 That the Overseers wait upon Mr Chetwynd & consult with him about removing the Black who is now in the Workhouse.

1817
      Dr Hawthorn's Bill for attending the Black   4. 2. 3
      Expenses of the Black man in the Workhouse   1. 14. 0

1819
      That the Churchwardens & Overseers be directed to lay a rate upon the different renters of the New Basin at Radford Bridge.

BIBLIOGRAPHY

The following books have been referred to in preparation of this book.

The Victorian History of the County of Stafford.
The Friendship of Cannock Chase by *M.Wright.*
A History of Staffordshire by *W.M.Greenslade and D.G.Stuart*
Cannock Forests from A History of Staffordshire.
Staffordshire Roads 1700-1840 *S.C.C.Education Dept.*
The Parish Church Magazines "The Three Decker"
The Priory of St.Thomas by *Rev.J.C.Dickenson*
Stafford Newsletter
Kelly's Directory 1850 to 1920
The Dissolution of the Monastries by *Rev.F.A.Hibbert*
Berkswich Parish Register 1601 to 1800
A Chartulary of St.Thomas Priory.
Records of the "Overseers of the Poor" and the Constablewick of Berkswich and Walton 1600 to 1800.
The Story of Berkswich by *members of W.I. 1949.*
Down Memory Lane by *Jim Foley.*
Down by Jacob's Ladder by *Laura Husselbee.*
Before the Houses Came by *Marjorie Knight.*